BELL'S CATHEDRALS:
THE CATHEDRAL CHURCH OF ROCHESTER

BELL'S CATHEDRALS:
THE CATHEDRAL CHURCH OF ROCHESTER

GEORGE HENRY PALMER

ISBN: 978-93-89679-70-0

Published: 1897

LECTOR HOUSE LLP
E-MAIL: lectorpublishing@gmail.com

SOUTH TRANSEPT FROM THE SOUTH-EAST

(From A Photograph By J. L. Allen).

BELL'S CATHEDRALS:
THE CATHEDRAL CHURCH OF ROCHESTER

A DESCRIPTION OF ITS FABRIC AND A BRIEF HISTORY OF THE EPISCOPAL SEE

BY

G. H. PALMER, B.A.

ARMS OF THE SEE

1897

GENERAL PREFACE.

This series of monographs has been planned to supply visitors to the great English Cathedrals with accurate and well illustrated guide books at a popular price. The aim of each writer has been to produce a work compiled with sufficient knowledge and scholarship to be of value to the student of archæology and history, and yet not too technical in language for the use of an ordinary visitor or tourist.

To specify all the authorities which have been made use of in each case would be difficult and tedious in this place. But amongst the general sources of information which have been almost invariably found useful are:—firstly, the great county histories, the value of which, especially in questions of genealogy and local records, is generally recognized; secondly, the numerous papers by experts which appear from time to time in the transactions of the antiquarian and archæological societies; thirdly, the important documents made accessible in the series issued by the Master of the Rolls; fourthly, the well-known works of Britton and Willis on the English Cathedrals; and, lastly, the very excellent series of Handbooks to the Cathedrals, originated by the late Mr. John Murray, to which the reader may in most cases be referred for fuller detail, especially in reference to the histories of the respective sees.

GLEESON WHITE.
EDWARD F. STRANGE.
Editors of the Series.

PREFACE.

Within the limits of a short preface it is impossible to enumerate all the sources of information, printed and in manuscript, to which reference has been made in the writing of this little work on the Cathedral church of the author's native city. He must especially mention the extent to which he has consulted the works of the Rev. G. M. Livett, Mr. W. H. St. John Hope, and Canon Scott Robertson among living authorities, while in the "Collections" made by Mr. Brenchley Rye, preserved in the British Museum (where Mr. Rye was once a keeper), notes have been found of many matters that might otherwise have escaped notice.

Most of the illustrations appear for the first time in this book. They are reproduced, by kind permission, from pen-drawings by Messrs. H. P. Clifford and R. J. Beale, and from photographs by Messrs. Horace Dan, J. L. Allen, F. G. M. Beaumont, and Messrs. Carl Norman and Co., of Tunbridge Wells.

Thanks are also due to the Very Rev. the Dean, the Rev. E. J. Nash, Mr. George Payne, F.S.A., and Mr. S. S. Brister, for kindnesses and helpful suggestions, as also to the head-verger, Mr. Miles, who, having been connected with the fabric for more than half a century, has a personal knowledge of its history during that time.

G. H. P.

9th Jan., 1897.

CONTENTS

Chapter   *Page*

GENERAL PREFACE.. vi

PREFACE. vii

I. HISTORY OF THE CATHEDRAL CHURCH OF CHRIST AND
THE BLESSED VIRGIN MARY. 1

II. THE EXTERIOR, MONASTIC BUILDINGS, ENCLOSURE, AND
GATES. 28

   • Tower and Bells 29

   • West Front 31

   • West Doorway. 34

   • Nave and Main Transept. .36

   • Choir and Gundulf's Tower 38

   • Monastic Buildings 40

   • Bishop's Palace 42

   • Enclosure and Gates 43

III. THE INTERIOR. 48

   • Nave 50

      » Lady Chapel 54

      » Main Transept 57

      » Font, Pulpit, and Stalls. 60

      » Monuments and Slabs 61

      » Stained Glass 63

   • North Choir Aisle. 64

   • Organ. 65

- Choir Screen 67
- Choir and Choir Transept 67
  - » Pavement 70
  - » Stalls 73
  - » Paintings 73
  - » Bishop's Throne 75
  - » Pulpit and Lectern 77
  - » Altar and Sedilia 77
  - » Communion Plate 80
  - » Monuments 80
  - » Stained Glass 86
  - » Chapter House Doorway 88
  - » Chapter House and Library 89
- South Choir Aisle 91
- Crypt 93

IV. THE DIOCESE AND BISHOPS 95

LIST OF ILLUSTRATIONS

Page

I. SOUTH TRANSEPT FROM THE SOUTH-EAST iv

II. ARMS OF THE SEE. v

III. THE WEST DOORWAY xii

IV. NORTH SIDE OF THE CATHEDRAL IN THE SEVEN-
TEENTH CENTURY 9

V. NORTH-WEST VIEW, EARLY EIGHTEENTH CENTURY 18

VI. NORTH-WEST VIEW, EARLY NINETEENTH CENTURY 22

VII. THE CATHEDRAL FROM THE CASTLE GARDENS 26

VIII. NORTH-EAST VIEW, WITH RUINS OF GUNDULF'S TOWER . .30

IX. CAPS OF WEST DOOR, NORTH SIDE 33

X. CAPS OF WEST DOOR, SOUTH SIDE. 34

XI. NEW CHAPTER ROOM AND RUINS OF THE OLD 41

XII. RUINS OF CLOISTERS, EAST RANGE 42

XIII. ARCHWAY IN THE ROMAN WALL. 44

XIV. THE PRIOR'S GATE IN 1825 45

XV. EASTGATE HOUSE, ROCHESTER. 47

XVI. PLAN OF ROCHESTER CATHEDRAL 49

XVII. THE NAVE, LOOKING WEST 52

XVIII. CAPITAL, SOUTH ARCADE OF NAVE 53

XIX. THE NAVE, LOOKING EAST. 55

XX. BAY OF NORMAN WORK IN NAVE 56

XXI.	THE NAVE FROM THE NORTH TRANSEPT	58
XXII.	THE SOUTH TRANSEPT	59
XXIII.	TOMB OF BISHOP HAMO DE HYTHE	66
XXIV.	THE CHOIR SCREEN: DEAN SCOTT MEMORIAL	68
XXV.	THE CHOIR, LOOKING EAST	69
XXVI.	CORBEL IN CHOIR (H. P. CLIFFORD DEL.).	71
XXVII.	A WINDOW, CHOIR CLERESTORY.	72
XXVIII.	WINDOW TRACERY, S. CHOIR TRANSEPT AISLE.	74
XXIX.	CORBEL IN CHOIR	75
XXX.	THE BISHOP'S THRONE	76
XXXI.	THE WHEEL OF FORTUNE	78
XXXII.	TOMB OF BISHOP JOHN DE SHEPPEY	84
XXXIII.	TOMBS OF BISHOPS GLANVILL AND ST. MARTIN	86
XXXIV.	CARVED COFFIN LID.	87
XXXV.	THE CHAPTER HOUSE DOORWAY	90
XXXVI.	TOMB OF BISHOP BRADFIELD	92
XXXVII.	THE CRYPT, LOOKING TO THE NORTH-EAST	93
XXXVIII.	THE GUILDHALL VANE	97

THE WEST DOORWAY

(From A Drawing By H. P. Clifford).

ROCHESTER CATHEDRAL.

CHAPTER I.

HISTORY OF THE CATHEDRAL CHURCH OF CHRIST AND THE BLESSED VIRGIN MARY.

Long, eventful, and very interesting is the history of the cathedral, or rather of the successive cathedrals, of the ancient city of Rochester. It is many centuries since, in 597, St. Augustine and his fellow missionaries landed on the coast of Thanet, almost on the very spot where Hengist and his bands had disembarked nearly one hundred and fifty years before. Hengist's descendant, Ethelbert, King of Kent, received them in the open air on the chalk downs above Minster, and, though he would not at once renounce the faith of his fathers, promised them shelter and protection. His conversion occurred a year later, and after that Christianity spread rapidly among his subjects. The royal city of Canterbury continued to be the centre of St. Augustine's labours, but only seven years passed, Bede tells us, ere he deemed it necessary to found other sees at Rochester and at London. Rochester therefore claims to be the second, or at most the third oldest of English bishoprics.

Justus, one of the band sent by St. Gregory to help the mission in 601, was consecrated as its first bishop in 604. A church was built for him by the king and dedicated to St. Andrew, the patron saint of the monastery on the Cælian Hill in Rome, from which St. Augustine and his companions had come. Bede relates that St. Paulinus was buried in it, later, "in secretario beati apostoli Andreæ quod rex Edilbertus a fundamentis in eadem Rhofi civitate construxit." Ethelbert endowed it with Priestfield (a large tract of land lying towards Borstal) which still belongs to it, and with other property; and Justus, though himself a monk, placed it in the hands of secular priests.

All traces of this Saxon cathedral disappeared long ago, and its exact site was forgotten and remained unknown until portions of its foundations were discovered in 1889, during the underpinning, preparatory to restoration, of the present west front.[1] Beneath this front, but only for a little way within it, the older foundations extended. They were of hard concrete, from 4 to 5 feet deep and wide, and still carried fragments of the walls, about 2 feet 4 inches wide, of tufa, sarsen, and Roman brick. These remains, on examination, proved to have belonged to the east end of a building, which, in this direction, terminated in an apse that occupied

---

[1] A full account by the Rev. G. M. Livett in Archæologia Cantiana, xviii.

almost the entire width. The southern junction of this apse was found first within the present church; and later, in lowering a gas main under the road outside, the north-east corner of the nave was discovered. The internal width of the building was then ascertained to be about 28 feet 6 inches. The lines of the north and south walls were followed by means of a probe across the old burial ground westwards as far as the road, running from the High Street to Boley Hill, and the foundations of the west wall lying along its side. These researches revealed no signs of aisles, quasi-transepts, or porch. If a western porch or apse ever existed, and has left any remains, these remains must lie beneath the road, so that excavation would be necessary to get at them. It has been conjectured that the west, as well as the east end, terminated apsidally. There would then have been placed, in the one apse, the high altar of St. Andrew, with the tombs of St. Paulinus, the apostle of Northumbria, and of St. Ythamar, the first Englishman to attain the episcopal dignity. Both of these died as bishops of Rochester, and they were buried in its cathedral in 644 and 655 respectively. The other apse, for this is possibly the right meaning to assign to "porticus" in the following quotation, would have contained the altar of St. Paul, and the tomb of Bishop Tobias, who is recorded to have been buried "in porticu Sancti Pauli apostoli, quam intra ecclesiam Sancti Andreæ sibi ipse in locum sepulchri fecerat." The tracing of the foundations of a straight wall at the west end proves nothing, I think, against the existence of this "porticus," be it porch or apse, beyond. We know that it was a later addition by Bishop Tobias himself, and it is not to be supposed that, when he cut away part of the old wall to unite his work to the building, he would have taken the trouble to dig beneath the surface and remove the foundations too. It is to be hoped that at some time in the future all the remains of the old Saxon church, under the burial ground and under the road, will be uncovered, and its complete plan thus, beyond all cavil, ascertained.

Troublous times fell on the church very soon after its erection, and, as Lambarde says: "No marvaile is it, if the glory of the place were not at any time very great, since on the one side the abilitie of the Bishops and the Chanons (inclined to advaunce it) was but meane, and on the other side the calamitie of fire and sworde (bent to destroy it) was in manner continuall." Even here in Kent a reaction against the new creed followed the death of Ethelbert, and his successor Eadbald relapsed into idolatry. Bishop Justus himself fled to Gaul in 617, and remained there a year before he was recalled by the king, but there were sadder times still to come. About the year 676, King Egbert having died, his brother Lothair usurped the throne of Kent. In this usurpation he devastated the country, without any respect for churches or religious houses, and especially plundered Rochester, driving Bishop Putta from his see. Soon afterwards, still within Lothair's reign, Ethelred of Mercia invaded Kent, "spoiled the whole Shyre, and laid this Citie waste."

There was little time to repair the losses and damages suffered on these occasions before the inroads of the Danes began. Rochester, lying at the head of an estuary on the side of England towards the Viking-land, was, of course, especially open to their attacks. In the year 840 they ravaged Kent, and both Canterbury and Rochester "felt the effects of their barbarity and hatred of the Christian religion." Again, in 884, large numbers of them, under Hasting, invaded England, but our city and cathedral were gloriously delivered out of their hands. "They," says Lambarde, "in the daies of King Alfred came out of Fraunce, sailed up the river of Medway to Rochester, and besieging the town, fortified over against it in such sorte that it was greatly distressed and like to have been yeelded, but that the King came speedily to the reskew and not onely raised the siege and delivered his subjects, but obtained also an honourable bootie of horses and captives that the besiegers had left behind them." Then, for a time, apparently, the city and cathedral had some repose, until, in 986, King Ethelred quarrelled with the bishop and besieged the town. In anger at its resistance he plundered the property of the church outside and had at last to be bought off. Much more grievous were the injuries and losses of about twelve years later, when, in 999, the Danes came again, drove away the inhabitants and plundered their city.

"And all these harmes Rochester received before the time of King William the Conqueror," in whose reign great changes for the better were to be begun.[2]

Siward, who had been bishop since 1058, retained the see, after the Conquest, until his death in 1075. Sad indeed was the condition of the cathedral then. It was itself "almost fallen to pieces from age," much of its property had been lost, and there were only four canons left. Even this small establishment was steeped in poverty; it is charged also with lack of zeal. Arnost, a monk of Bec, succeeded Siward, but he died within a year. A bishop had now to be chosen who would be competent to cope with the poverty and deficiencies of the see, and to carry through remedial measures. At last Lanfranc appointed Gundulf, of whose great capacity he had personal knowledge. Want of money at first stood in the way of reforms; but, with the archbishop's help, much of the alienated property of the see was recovered, and the substitution of regular for secular clergy was undertaken. In 1082 a priory was established with twenty monks of the Order of St. Benedict, a number which grew to sixty before Gundulf's death. It was necessary, now, that a new church should be built, for the old one was not only, as has been said, very dilapidated, but also, probably, too small for the new establishment.

One of Gundulf's first undertakings seems to have been the erection, about 150 feet to the east of the Saxon cathedral, of the strong tower bearing his name. Ruins of this are still to be seen on the north side of the choir (see p. 52). It was about the year 1080 that he began his church. The plan was cruciform, but not of the usual northern type. The eastern arm was six bays long, and had aisles of the same length as the presbytery; its four easternmost bays stood on an undercroft, of which a portion still remains in the present crypt. The excavations there, in 1881, uncovering the old foundations, proved that the shape of this end of the church used to be rectangular and not apsidal. It had been concluded that its form was such, but on less positive grounds, thirty years before. The whole arm was 76 feet long by 60 wide, and from its end there was a small rectangular projection, constructed, probably, for the relics of St. Paulinus, which Gundulf, or, according to another account, Lanfranc, transported from the older church. In this prolongation we seem to have a germ of those that gave us afterwards the Lady Chapels of Li-

---

[2] For Norman work, see the paper by Mr. W. H. St. John Hope in Archæologia, xlix., and Mr. Ashpitel's earlier essay in Jour. of the Brit. Archæol. Assoc., ix.

chfield, Westminster, Gloucester, and elsewhere. This small excrescence, chapel it can scarcely be called, probably did not rise very high, as room had to be left above it for the east window, which, with the clerestory, was needed to light the presbytery. The latter, like the choir of the present cathedral and like that of St. Alban's, had its aisles divided from it by solid walls.

To the west of the six bays of the eastern arm crossed a transept, remarkable for its narrowness. In the angle between it and the south wall of the choir, rose, as an integral part of the building, a smaller tower balancing the earlier great one of Gundulf, which had been allowed to remain in an almost similar, but independent, position on the other side. It has been conjectured that the lower portions of these two towers formed the transepts of Gundulf's church. This would have greatly reduced the length of its choir, while adding, to the same amount, to that of its nave. Such a theory is, however, quite untenable now, as the real lines of the transept have been traced. In 1872, when the south end of the present transept was underpinned, parts of the foundations of its predecessor's east and south walls were uncovered, and the footings of the clasping pilaster buttress of its south-west angle exposed. These showed that the transept occupied the position which we have assigned to it, and that its entire length was 120 feet, while it was only 14 feet wide. This width being so small, it is probable that the arcading of the nave was continued right up to the choir arch. There was no tower over the crossing. Of a south tower, as has been mentioned, the foundations have been found, but the only signs of it now left above ground seem to be some tufa quoins in the wall by the cloister door. Even if these traces did not remain there would be ample documentary evidence to prove that it had once existed.

The nave and its aisles were intended to be at least nine bays long. In the underpinning of the side aisles in 1875-76, the bases of Gundulf's buttresses were discovered, his foundations being easily distinguishable from later ones, and the curious fact was then made manifest that he did not finish the nave westwards. On the south side his work stops half a bay from the present west front, and on the north it only extends three bays to the west of the present transept. It is interesting to note that it is just from this point that it was, in the seventeenth century, found necessary to start the rebuilding of a portion of the north aisle wall. Taking it for granted that the nave arcades were, after the old English traditional manner, continued to the choir arch, we conclude that Gundulf completed nine arches on the south and five on the north side. The bishop probably finished the south aisle that he might build the cloister and monastic buildings against it in their usual positions; but did not deem the north so important, as it would be of no such ulterior use. In the same way the choir was finished, while the nave, or parochial portion, in which the monastic establishment had less interest, was possibly left to the townsmen, and remained longer incomplete. All that the monks most wanted,—enough of the nave to secure the stability of the choir and transepts, and the south wall that supported their cloister,—was built under Gundulf's direction. It has been thought likely that the nave was completed by the parishioners before the later Norman period. If so, the builders of that time seem to have swept away all the townsmen's work, probably because of its ruder execution.

Gundulf's arcades consisted, apparently, of two plain square-edged orders; the plan of his piers is not known. We do not seem to have any of his work, now, above the first string course in the nave. The triforium, in its present form at any rate, is, like the casing of the piers and the outer decorated order of the arches, of later Norman work.

The cathedral, or rather the part described above as Gundulf's work, seems to have been erected by 1087, in which year William the Conqueror bequeathed some money, robes, and ornaments to it. The monastic portions were certainly finished before Lanfranc's death in 1089.

Lambarde, following perhaps the chronicler who said, "Ecclesiam Andreæ, pæne vetustate dirutam, novam ex integro, ut hodie apparet, ædificavit," does not seem to suspect the incompleteness of Gundulf's work of which he gives the following quaint account. He tells how he "re-edified the great church at Rochester, erected the Priorie, and where as he founde but half a dozen secular priests" (the older authority that we have followed makes it still worse, only mentioning four) "in the Church at his comming, he never ceased, till he had brought together at the least three score Monkes into the place. Then removed he the dead bodies of his predecessors, and with great solemnitie translated them into this newe work: and there also Lanfranc was present with his purse, and of his owne charge in-coffened in curious worke of cleane silver the body of Paulinus, ... to the which shrine there was afterwarde (according to the superstitious maner of those times) much concourse of people and many oblations made. Besides this, they both joined in suite to the King, and not onely obtained restitution of sundry the possessions witholden from the church, but also procured, by his liberalitie and example, newe donations of many other landes and privileges. To be short, Gundulphus (over-living Lanfranc) never rested building and begging, tricking and garnishing, till he had advaunced this his creature, to the just wealth, beautie, and estimation of a right Popish Priorie."

Subsequently the choir was re-arranged; and the nave partly rebuilt, partly re-faced, added to, and finished with the west front, which, to a great extent, still remains. This later Norman work was carried out from east to west during the episcopates of Ernulf (1115-24) and John of Canterbury (1125-37). The upper part of the west front and some of the carving may not have been completed within even that period. What seems certain is, that we are indebted to later Norman builders for the re-casing of the piers of the nave arcade, the greater richness of their capitals, the outer decorated order of the arches, the triforium with its richly diapered tympana, and the west front. Assigning most of these works to the time of Bishop John, as seems best, we can point to others that testify to Ernulf's architectural skill. He is recorded to have built the refectory, dormitory, and chapter house. Portions of these still remain, and one feature, in the ornamentation of the chapter house, especially marks it as his work. This is a peculiar lattice-like diaper, which occurs elsewhere at Rochester, — in fragments that belonged probably to a beginning by him of the renovation of the choir, — but has only been noticed at one other place: by the entrance to the crypt at Canterbury, where also it is due to him.

An indication of the completion of the church in this new form, — or rather, it is safer to say, of the final destruction of its Saxon predecessor,—is perhaps contained in an entry that has been found, that "Bishop John translated the body of St. Ythamar, Bishop of Rochester." It seems peculiar that this relic was not moved to the new church at the same time as the remains of St. Paulinus. It may be that the earlier Norman bishop and monks valued the greatest of St. Augustine's fellow missionaries—a foreigner, like themselves, working here for the church—more highly than his successor in the bishopric and fellow saint, who belonged to the recently conquered and still despised English, and whose great glory was that of being the first bishop of their race.

The cathedral was apparently dedicated in 1130, by the Archbishop William de Corbeuil assisted by thirteen bishops, but one authority gives 1133 as the date. In "The history and antiquities of Rochester"[3] we read: "The city was honoured with a royal visit in the year 1130, when Henry I., the Archbishop of Canterbury, and many of the nobility were present at the consecration of St. Andrew's Church, then just finished: but their mirth was turned into sorrow, by their being mournful spectators of a dreadful conflagration which broke out on the 7th of May, and, without any regard to the majesty of the king, grandeur of the church, or solemnity of the occasion, laid the city in ashes and much damaged the new church." The Chronicle says, as to the extent of the damage done by this fire, "Civitas pene tota conflagravit."

The Rochester chronicler, Edmund de Hadenham, records two great fires under the years 1138 and 1177; Gervase also mentions these, but gives their dates as 1137 and 1179. The exact extent of the damage and consequent repairs is not known in the case of either. It would seem from Edmund de Hadenham's account of the earlier, that, in it, the offices suffered most; and he speaks of their restoration under Bishop Ascelin. We read that the monks had to find other quarters, for a time, for many of their number whom it had rendered homeless. Gervase says of the same fire, "combusta est Ecclesia S. Andreæ Roffensis et tota civitas cum officinis Episcopi et monachorum," and of the later one that in it the church, with the offices, was burnt and reduced to a cinder.

Lambarde, staunch Protestant as he was, saw in these fires a token of God's disapproval of such monastic institutions. After telling of the foundation by Gundulf, he continues, "but God (who moderating all things by his divine providence, shewed himselfe alwaies a severe visitour of these irreligious Synagogues) God (I say) set fire on this building twise within the compasse of one hundreth yeeres after the erection of the same." He then goes on to attribute the quarrels between Bishop Gilbert de Glanvill and the monks, and the church's losses through these, and its spoliation by King John's troops, to the same divine judgment. His book contains a great amount of accurate information, but often, as here, and in his account, quoted above, of Gundulf's really good and useful work, shows the strong prejudices of the ordinary English Protestant of his time.

In one or other of these two fires the eastern arm and transepts of Gundulf's fabric, and Ernulf's conventual buildings, must have been much injured if not re-

[3] Anonymous, but probably by the Rev. S. Denne and W. Shrubsole. Published in 1772; second edition, 1817.

duced to ruins, and to the date of the second the outer part of the north choir aisle possibly belongs. Probably about 1190, Gilbert de Glanvill, who was Bishop of Rochester from 1185 to 1214, built a new cloister and the lower part of the outer wall of the south choir aisle as a portion of it. A great deal of work was done about that time to the conventual buildings by different priors and monks. Many records relating to it are gathered together in Mr. Ashpitel's paper.[4] He evidently thought that the church was then neglected—though, as we shall see, it does not seem to have been so—and apologizes for the monks, pointing out that there must have been enough of the nave left for services, and that, this being the case, it was natural for them, in their almost complete homelessness, to think of their dormitories, etc., before anything else.

The development, by means of great additions and alterations, of the present eastern arm and its magnificent crypt from the earlier and smaller Norman structures was probably taken in hand about 1190. The new work seems to have been begun from the east and continued westwards. It was at first perhaps roofed temporarily with wood, and only vaulted later. It may have been far enough advanced to allow of William of Perth's burial, directly after his death in 1201, in the north choir transept (still called by his name), where his tomb and shrine were afterwards so much resorted to. On the other hand, his body may have been laid in the north choir aisle until the new transept was ready to receive it. This was probably not the case however; it certainly was not, if the conjecture be correct, that 1195 is the approximate date of the removal of the eastern half of the Norman undercroft and of the portion of the presbytery above it, and that a little work in the choir aisles had been done even earlier. Other authorities, though, incline to the opinion that the part of the Norman presbytery which projected into the new work was not removed before it was almost completely inclosed. This would put off its demolition till later.

· The "whole choir" was, we read, rebuilt by William de Hoo, the sacrist, with the offerings at St. William's tomb. The word "choir" must here, of course, be used in its more restricted sense, meaning the choir proper, as distinct from its transept and the presbytery. Even then to say absolutely that he rebuilt it is to go too far, for the walls dividing it from its aisles are still in the main of Norman construction, though they have Early English facings and decorations, and additions of this later period to their upper parts. The original intention of the architect had apparently been to change into arcades these solid walls, but, if so, he abandoned it. When the work on the choir walls was finished, some re-modelling of its aisles was soon carried out, buttresses being built within them to withstand the thrust of the new vaulting of the central part. In William de Hoo's work at this time we must include the arches across the western ends of the choir aisles, with the one bay of the transept clerestory over the northern of them, and possibly also the choir arch, with the piers that carry it. It seems, however, that these piers were only finally freed from the Norman nave arcade, and completed, as we now have them, to be the eastern pair of supports to the central tower, by Richard de Eastgate about twenty

---

[4] For Norman work, see the paper by Mr. W. H. St. John Hope in Archæologia, xlix., and Mr. Ashpitel's earlier essay in Jour. of the Brit. Archæol. Assoc., ix.

years later. It is recorded that the new work had been roofed and leaded by the sacrist Radulfus de Ros and the prior Helias. The new choir was first used in 1227, when the monks made their solemn entry into it, and the works, that have been described above, must have been finished at that date. Some fittings, probably originally inserted at this early period, still remain, viz., the eastern side of the pulpitum and some woodwork preserved in the present stalls. Richard de Wendover, Bishop of Rochester, and Richard, Bishop of Bangor, dedicated the church, or rather its new portions, but it was not until 1240 that the ceremony took place.

We must now go back a few years in order to mention the great losses that the cathedral sustained in 1215. In that year King John besieged and captured Rochester Castle, stoutly held against him by William de Albinet and other powerful barons. Then, Edmund de Hadenham tells us, the church was so plundered that there was not a pyx left "in which the body of the Lord might rest upon the altar." At such a time the offerings at St. William's tomb, which have been alluded to above, were especially needed and especially acceptable.

Within the first half of the thirteenth century, but certainly several years later than the entry into the choir, further great works were begun by the monk and sacrist Richard de Eastgate. He probably commenced by clearing away the two eastern arches of each of the nave arcades, which, it will be remembered, are thought to have been continued right up to the choir arch; and, then, having completed the piers at the ends of the choir walls, laid the bases of the two others that with them support the central tower. He next began the new north transept (*ala borealis versus portam beati Willelmi*), and made it half as wide again as its slender predecessor. Afterwards the north-west tower pier was erected at the junction of the transept and the nave, and, finally, there is a discussion as to whether the northern tower arch was built now or not until later. We are told that all this work, begun by Richard de Eastgate, was almost finished by Thomas de Mepeham, who became sacrist in 1255. The laying out of the bases of the western pair of piers to the central tower was formerly assigned to a much earlier date; while the eastern piers were supposed to have been finally finished in William de Hoo's time. This work would, however, scarcely have been done before the new wider transept was undertaken, and it cannot have been carried out before the eastern part of the Norman nave was cleared away.

Only a short time elapsed then before the building of the south transept (*ala australis versus curiam*) by Richard de Waldene, monk and sacrist, and next came the completion of the supports for the central tower, by the construction of its south-west pier and the other arches. The building of the eastern (the choir) arch, and the possible earlier date of the northern one, have already been spoken of. The two bays of the nave nearest the crossing, were also rebuilt in their present form, and the stability of the arches that were to bear the central tower was thus secured. The reconstruction of the whole nave seems to have been intended by the architects of this time; but want of funds, probably, stopped the work.

NORTH SIDE OF THE CATHEDRAL IN THE SEVENTEENTH CENTURY
(From An Engraving By Daniel King).

To leave purely architectural history for a while, we find the church on which all this labour was so lovingly bestowed undergoing another terrible experience in 1264. On Good Friday of that year it was desecrated by the troops of Simon de Montfort, after their capture of the city. In the old annalist's account we read (in Latin) how they "entered the church of St. Andrew on the day on which the Lord hung on the cross for sinners.... Armed knights on their horses, coursing around the altars, dragged away with impious hands some who fled for refuge thither, the gold and silver and other precious things being with violence carried off thence. Many royal charters, too, and other muniments, in the Prior's Chapel, and necessary to the church of Rochester, were destroyed and torn up. The oratories, cloisters, chapter house, infirmary and all the sacred buildings were turned into horses' stables, and everywhere filled with the dung of animals and the defilement of dead bodies."

There is a record of a later, more welcome visit from Earl Simon's conqueror. In 1300 Edward I. made a progress in Kent, and we find the following items in the wardrobe accounts for this, the twenty-eighth year of his reign. On the 18th of February he offered seven shillings at the shrine of St. William, and a like amount again on the next day. He then went forward to Canterbury, and on his return from the archiepiscopal city gave, on the 27th of the same month, seven shillings each for the shrines of SS. Paulinus and Ythamar in the church of the Priory.

From March till October, 1314, we read that Isabel, the queen of Robert Bruce, was a prisoner in Rochester Castle, permitted to walk at convenient times, under safe custody, within its precincts and those of the Priory of St. Andrew adjoining. This is, however, to some extent a matter of controversy.

The fourteenth century saw the junction of the new and the Norman work in the nave completed, and the design of rebuilding the whole western arm finally abandoned. A beautiful capital at the joining on the south side will call for especial mention later, and in the part of the triforium just over it there is a piece of apparently later-Norman work, which is, however, by builders of the "Decorated" period. They seem to have found it best to reproduce here, as accurately as possible, what they had just destroyed. That it is by them is shown by the stone used, which is greensand and not the Caen stone of later-Norman workmen, and by differences in working. The early-Norman architects had chiefly used tufa, and these successive changes of material are of great help in assigning their respective dates to various parts of the fabric.

About 1320 some alterations were made in the clerestory of the south transept, while on its east side there was, apparently, a conversion of two arches into one to form a large altar recess. This change seems to be alluded to when in 1322 the altar of the Blessed Virgin Mary in this transept is spoken of as "de nova constructo." At this time there were many disputes between the monks and the parishioners of St. Nicholas, whose altar[5] stood from 1322, at any rate, till 1423, against the rood-screen across the end of the nave beneath the western tower-arch. In 1327, in which year Mr. Walcott tells of a riotous assault by the townsfolk on the pretence of a right of entrance by day or night for the ministration of the Viaticum, an oratory was built, by agreement between the monks and the parishioners, "in

[5] For further information about this altar, see p. 52-53.

angulo navis," for the Reserved Sacrament, and the small door was inserted in the west front. To dread of such attacks or fear of the crowds of strangers constantly passing through the town, which stood on the main road to Canterbury and the Continent, we must attribute the erection of the screens and strong doors of this time, which shut off the choir from the rest of the cathedral, and also the almost contemporaneous walling off of the priory from the town. Among these screens is included the west side of the pulpitum, which still contains its original central doorway, as well as the screens in the choir aisles. To this same period also belongs, apparently, the western cloister door.

In 1343 the central tower was at last raised by Bishop Hamo de Hythe, and capped by him with a wooden spire in which he placed four bells named Dunstan, Paulinus, Ythamar, and Lanfranc. The south tower had already been destroyed and with its demolition we approach the end of the changes which have brought the south choir aisle to its present form and which will be described in the chapter on the interior of the church.[6] The completion of this aisle is assigned to W. de Axenham; its wooden roof seems to belong to King Edward II.'s time. Decorated tracery was inserted in the presbytery windows soon after the erection of the tower, and Bishop Hamo is recorded to have reconstructed in marble and alabaster the shrines of SS. Paulinus and Ythamar. Finally, to this time, to about the middle of the fourteenth century, belongs the beautiful doorway which leads to the present chapter room and library, and is one of the chief glories of the church.

In the painted decoration of the choir walls, with its alternate lions and fleurs-de-lis, — which Sir Gilbert Scott partly saved and partly renewed, — we have probably a contemporary allusion to and commemoration of, the victories won by our countrymen in France in Edward III.'s reign. Rochester lay on the main route to the Continent and is sure to have seen much of the soldiers who passed to and fro. In 1360 there is a record of the passage of John II. on his way back to his own land. He had, it will be remembered, been defeated by the Black Prince at Poictiers in 1356, and brought as a prisoner to England until arrangements should be made for his ransom. It was on the 2nd of July that he went through the town, and, ere he left it, made an offering of sixty crowns at the Church of St. Andrew.

The oratory that was constructed in 1327, and other attempted arrangements, did not settle the differences between the monks and the parishioners of St. Nicholas. These were only finally ended by the erection of a new church, for the use of the latter, in the cemetery called the Green Church Haw, on the north side of the cathedral. The people were still allowed to pass within the north side of the cathedral in their processions, and the Perpendicular doorway which exists, walled up, towards the west end of the north aisle wall, was inserted for their passage. The right that the mayor and corporation of the city still retain of entering the cathedral in their robes and with their maces, etc., borne before them, by the great west door, seems to be a relic of the old parochial use of the nave.

Later in the fifteenth century the clerestory and vaulting of the north choir aisle were finished, and Perpendicular windows were inserted in the nave aisles. Then, about 1470, the great west window was inserted, and the nave clerestory,

[6] See p. 91-92.

together with the northern pinnacle of the west gable, rebuilt. It was in 1490, or thereabouts, apparently, that the Perpendicular builders carried out their last important work: the erection of the so-called Lady Chapel, in the corner between the south transept and the nave. This seems to be really an extension of the Lady Chapel in the south transept (where the altar to the Blessed Virgin Mary has been already mentioned), to be a nave to this rather than a chapel itself.

There is now nothing very important to record until we come to the time, when, at the suppression of the monasteries by Henry VIII., regulars, after more than four centuries and a half, ceased at last to form the establishment of this cathedral. Two general visitations of religious houses had been made in 1535 and 1537, but neither of the reports on this establishment seems to be extant. If either could be found it would very possibly prove unfavourable. Some injunctions by Bishop Wells, in 1439, nearly a century before, seem to show that he found deviations from the rule of the order, and that he thought precautions against its infraction necessary.

During its later days the priory does not seem to have been in a flourishing state. In the twentieth year of King Henry VIII.'s reign, the annual income of its estates was returned to the exchequer as only £486 11s. 6d., and its financial condition, though it has not been accurately ascertained, seems to have been bad. In 1498 there were only twenty-four monks in the house, though the original establishment had been sixty, and this great diminution in numbers was probably due to the want of funds. Later, to the priory's acknowledgment of the Royal Supremacy, dated June 10th, 1534, there were only twenty signatures altogether.

The 20th of March, 1540, is the date of the commission to the Archbishop of Canterbury, George Lord Cobham, and others to accept the surrender of the house and its possessions to the king. On the 8th of April following the seal of the convent was affixed to the instrument of resignation, a document which seems to us very ironical in its wording. It was sent in, we read by them "with their unanimous assent and consent, deliberately and of their own certain knowledge and mere motion, from certain just and reasonable causes, especially moving their minds and consciences, of their own free will." Some pensions were granted on the day of surrender, the total number given among the dispersed monks being thirteen. These seem very few, but possibly vacancies had been left unfilled for some years in dread of such an event, and perhaps one or two of the monks embraced the opportunity of release from their vows. Others, we know, were given new appointments. Even the above small number soon dwindled. In Cardinal Pole's list of 1556 we find only one former member of this priory recorded as in receipt of an annuity, and five as in receipt of pensions. The annuity was possibly a payment to which the house was already liable at the time of the suppression, while the pensions would be the "convenient charity" of the Crown.

When enforcing their surrender the king had said that the monks were to go, that the endowment they had so long possessed "might be tornyd to better use as heraffter shall folow, werby Gods word myght the better be sett forthe, cyldren brought up in learning, clerks nuryshyd in the universites," etc. We shall now see how he tried to secure this improvement, and how, in some respects, at any rate, his scheme was good. It was not hurried forth at once, the letters patent for the new establishment not being issued till the 20th of June, 1542. It was then incorporated under the title of "the Dean and Chapter of the Cathedral Church of Christ and the Blessed Virgin Mary of Rochester."[7] Provision was made for a dean, six prebendaries, six minor canons, a deacon, a sub-deacon, six lay clerks, a master of the choristers, eight choristers, an upper and an under master of the grammar school, twenty scholars, six poor men, a porter, who was also to be barber, a butler, a chief cook, and an assistant. A yearly pension of £5 was to be paid also to four scholars, of whom two were to be members of each University.

The offices of deacon and sub-deacon were disused after the Reformation, and the butler and cooks ceased to be appointed when there was no longer a common table. Charles I. attached one of the prebends to the archdeaconry of Rochester in 1637; a union which is still maintained. Another was annexed by letters patent of 1713 to the provostship of Oriel College, Oxford, and this connection was confirmed by Parliament in the same year, though it has, of course, to lapse when, as has been the case, the provost is a layman. On the whole, the establishment, thus originally provided for, is maintained, but the full numbers are not just now kept up throughout, owing to a great loss of income due to the gradual decrease in value of landed property. With regard to the educational provisions, it will, perhaps, be interesting just to mention here, that it was chiefly owing to the late Rev. R. Whiston, long the head master of the Rochester Grammar School, that this and similar institutions were, about the middle of this century, made to conform more to the spirit of their original foundations, by the making of alterations, especially in the terms of scholarships, to meet the great changes that have since occurred in money values.

In 1541 panelled book-desks were provided for the new canons and singing men. Some of the panels belonging to them still remain, and are incorporated in the present choir stalls.

For some years little of interest occurred directly concerning the cathedral itself, though much happened of importance in the history of the see and its bishops. In 1558, however, the body of Cardinal Pole lay here for a night in state, and we are able to give an eye-witness's account, written by Francis Thynne, afterwards Lancaster Herald, and published in Holinshed's Chronicles in 1587. "Cardinal Poole died the same daie wherein the Queene" (Mary) "died, the third hour of the night.... His bodie was first conveyed from Lambeth to Rochester, where it rested one night, being brought into the Church of Rochester at the West doore, not opened manie yeres before. At what time myselfe, then a yoong scholer" (he was born in 1545), "beheld the funeral pompe thereof, which trulie was great and answerable both to his birth and calling, with store of burning torches and mourning weedes. At what time, his coffin, being brought into the church, was covered with a cloth of blacke velvet, with a great crosse of white satten over all the length and bredth of the same, in the middest of which crosse his Cardinal's hat was placed. From Rochester he was conveied to Canterbury, where the same bodie (being first before it came to Rochester inclosed in lead) was, after three daies spent in

---

[7] The original dedication was to St. Andrew.

his commendations set foorth in Latine and English, committed to the earth in the Chapell of Thomas Becket."

In 1568 we have a curious story, said to be taken originally from records in the Rochester Diocesan Registry of the discovery and apprehension, at Rochester, of a Jesuit in disguise. A certain Thomas Heth, purporting to be a poor minister, came and asked the dean to recommend him for some preferment. The dean said that he would consider his case after he had heard him preach before him in the cathedral. No fault seems to have been found with the sermon, but in the pulpit afterwards, the sexton, Richard Fisher, picked up a letter that had been dropped, and carried it to the bishop, Dr. Gest. This was directed to Th. Finne from Samuel Malta, a noted Jesuit at Madrid. Heth was brought up and examined before the bishop; he acknowledged that he had preached for six years in England, but said that he had left the hated order. He was then remanded until the case had been reported to the queen and her council. Incriminating papers were in the meantime found among his belongings, and, at a later second examination, he confessed. He was pilloried, branded, and mutilated after the cruel manner of those days, beside the High Cross at Rochester, and was condemned to be imprisoned for life. From this imprisonment he was released by an early death.

We are next able to mention a visit by Good Queen Bess. She came to Rochester during her summer progress in Kent in 1573, and lodged, during her first four days in the city, at the Crown Inn. On the last day of her stay she was entertained by Mr. Richard Watts at his house, on Boley Hill, which then, it is said, obtained its name of "Satis," she having answered with this word his apologies for the poor accommodation that he had been able to offer to so great a queen. On Sunday, the 19th of September, she attended divine service, and heard a sermon at the cathedral.

In 1591 there is recorded the destruction of a great part of the chancel by fire, but the fabric itself does not seem to have been much damaged. At any rate, in 1607 the dean and chapter were able to certify to Archbishop Abbot, who was making a metropolitical visitation, that the church, though requiring weekly repair from its antiquity, was, as a whole, in reasonable condition. This statement was probably accurate, as the return was not followed by any injunctions from the visitor.

During the preceding year, A.D. 1606, Christian IV. of Denmark, brother-in-law of James I., had visited Rochester in company with the latter King and Queen Anne, and their eldest son, Prince Henry. These royal personages had separate lodgings during their stay, King James's own being at the Bishop's house. It was on Saturday that they arrived, and "the next day," we are told, "being Sunday, ... their Majesties came to the Cathedrall Church of the Colledge, where they heard a most learned sermon by a reverende grave and learned Doctor." This was Dr. Parry, Dean of Chester, one of the most famous preachers at his time. King Christian is said to have been much pleased with his discourse, and to have given him afterwards a very rich ring. The royal travellers then visited the shipping, and on the Monday "set forwarde towardes Gravesend."

In Archbishop Laud's annual report on the diocese to King Charles I., in 1633, it is said that the Bishop (Dr. John Bowle) complained "that the cathedral suffered much for want of glass in the windows, and the churchyard lay very indecently, and the gates down, because the dean and chapter refused to be visited by him on pretence that the statutes were not confirmed under the broad seal." Here the king wrote in the margin: "This must be remedied one way or other, concerning which I expect a particular account of you." There was probably a considerable likelihood then of the imposition of a new set of statutes of the archbishop's devising; the dean and chapter, however, managed to retain the old ones. They submitted to a visit from the archbishop, as metropolitan, in the following year, and in answer to one of his questions stated that the cathedral was sufficiently repaired in all its parts, the only defects, and these small, being in the glass of some of the windows. These defects had been left for a little while, owing to the great charges that they had incurred of late years. If they had been among the first parts repaired they would probably have wanted mending again before the other works were finished. This would have involved more expense. In addition to their ordinary annual outlay on the fabric, they had recently expended on it and on the "making of the organs" more than £1,000. The archbishop evidently thought this report correct, for with regard to the cathedral and its furniture he only found it necessary to enjoin: that the windows should be repaired without delay in a decent manner, and the bells together with the frames put in good order; that there should be a new fair desk in the choir, and new church books provided without delay; that the communion table should be placed at the east end of the choir in a decent manner, and a fair rail put up to go across the choir as in other cathedral churches. That they had not of their own accord seen to what he considered such an important matter as this last, is sure to have influenced him against them. In their answer the dean and chapter said that all these things were either done, or would be taken in hand as soon as possible, but pointed out that, if the altar were removed quite to the end, the clergyman ministering at it would be almost out of hearing of the congregation, and suggested instead the erection of a screen behind it, in the more westerly position, where it then was and again is, for it to stand against. This suggestion seems not to have been accepted. They pointed out the impossibility of carrying out his injunctions as to the "verie handsome fence" for their churchyard. They had before told him of parochial rights, and rights of way, in the cemetery, and promised that it should be as decently kept as possible in the future, and that they would report the mayor and citizens if they also did not do their best in the matter. The maintenance of the establishment seems to have been generally satisfactory, but there was some discussion as to requiring a "pettie canon" and two lay clerks, who were "gent, of his Ma[ties] chappell," to provide substitutes when they were at court. The new desk was taken in hand, but they said: "for our church bookes, we conceave that noe church in England hath newer or fayerer," and went on to give particulars. As to his enforcement of the wearing of "square cappes" within the cathedral at times of service and sermons, they said that this was the usual practice of the dean and canons in residence, and that care would be taken that it should now be carried out by all.[8]

---

[8] These answers are published in the Fourth Report of the Historical Manuscripts Commission.

In Lansdowne MS. no. 213, at the British Museum, there is included "A relation of a short survey of the westerne counties of England, ... observed in a seven weekes journey begun at Norwich and thence into the West on Thursday, August 4th, 1635, ... by the same Lieutenant, that, with the Captaine and Ancient (Ensign) of the military company in Norwich, made a journey into the North the yeere before." It includes an interesting, rather antithetical, account by this officer of Rochester and its cathedral as they were just before the troublous times of the Civil War. He says: "As I found this Citty little and sweet, so I found her cheife and best structures correspondent to her smallnesse, which was neat and hansome, and neither great nor sumptuous. And first I'le begin with her cheife seat the Cathedrall, which was consecrated in Hen. the I. time; and though the same be but small and plaine, yet it is very lightsome and pleasant: her quire is neatly adorn'd with many small pillars of marble; her organs though small yet are they rich and neat; her quiristers though but few, yet orderly and decent." He then passes on to the deanery, the episcopal palace, and the monuments in the church. He names some of these last, and alludes to "diverse others also of antiquity, so dismembred, defac'd and abused as I was forced to leave them to some better discovery than I was able to render of them; as also the venerable shrine of St. William." John Weever, whose "Ancient funerall Monuments" was published in 1631, agrees with our Norwich lieutenant as to the dilapidated state of the older monuments in the church in his time. People are at times found, who thoughtlessly charge the Roundheads with all such defacements as these, but the above authorities clear them in many cases, though still leaving acts of "vandalism" that they are responsible for.

In "A perfect diurnall of the severall passages in our late Journey into Kent, from Aug. 19 to Sept. 3, 1642, by the appointment of both Houses of Parliament" we have an official account of the doings of the Parliamentary soldiers in this cathedral as elsewhere in the county. Of the last day of their stay in the town on their outward journey, we read: "On Wednesday, being Bartholomew Day, before we marched forth, some of our souldiers (remembring their protestation which they tooke) went to the Cathedrall about 9 or 10 of the clock, in the midst of their superstitious worship, with their singing men and boys; they (owing them no reverence) marched up to the place where the altar stood, and staying awhile, thinking they would have eased their worship, and demanded a reason of their posture, but seeing they did not, the souldiers could not forbeare any longer to wait upon their pleasure, but went about the worke they came for. First they removed the Table to its place appointed, and then tooke the seate which it stood upon, being made of deale board, having 2 or 3 steps to go up to the altar, and brake that all to pieces; it seemed the altar was so holy that the ground was not holy enough to stand upon. This being done they pluckt down the rails and left them for the poore to kindle their fires; and so left the organs to be pluckt down when we came back again, but it appeared before we came back they tooke them downe themselves. When this work was finished we then advanced towards Maidstone." At Canterbury it was far worse. There, "on Saterday morning before we departed some of our souldiers visited the great Cathedrall, and made havock of all their Popish reliques.... When they had done their pleasure we all marched to Dover." Their pleasure meant terrible injuries to this grand church.

The Cavaliers themselves agree that Rochester Cathedral suffered far less mischief than many other sacred edifices, from the bigotry of their opponents. The following passage, from a paper entitled "Mercurius Rusticus," of 1647, is quoted in "The History and Antiquities of Rochester." "In September, 1640" (apparently a mistake for August—September, 1642) "the rebels coming to Rochester, brought the same affections which they express'd at Canterbury; but in wisdom thought it not safe to give them scope here, as there; for the multitude, tho' mad enough yet were not so mad, nor stood so prepared to approve such heathenish practices. By this means the monuments of the dead, which elsewhere they brake up and violated, stood untouch'd; escocheons and arms of the nobility and gentry remained undefaced; the seats and stalls of the quire escaped breaking down; only those things which were wont to stuff up parliamentary petitions, and were branded by the leaders of the faction for popery and innovations; in these they took liberty to let loose their wild zeal: they brake down the rails about the Lord's table or altar; they seized upon the velvet of the holy table; and, in contempt of those holy misteries which were celebrated on the table, removed the table itself into a lower part of the church. To conclude with this farther addition, as I am credibly informed, they so far profaned this place as to make use of it in the quality of a tippling place, as well as dug several saw-pits, and the city joiners made frames for houses in it." Even the Royalist and Church party, therefore, allow that comparatively little damage was done here. The statement that the monuments "stood untouch'd" is especially interesting and valuable as coming from them.

The name of one despoiler is on record. In the answer by the dean and chapter to an enquiry by Bishop Warner, a certain John Wyld, a shoemaker of Rochester, is mentioned as having taken down and sold iron and brass work from some of the tombs. The Rev. S. Denne gives the following additional information,—on the testimony of "Mr. William Head, senior alderman of the city, a very antient worthy man, who died March 5, 1732,"—that the church was used as a stable by Fairfax's troops, who turned their horses' heads into the stalls in the choir.

Great efforts were made directly after the Restoration to bring the building into a decent state once more. On the 10th of April, 1661, Samuel Pepys, then on a visit of inspection to Chatham as Secretary to the Admiralty, tells, in his diary, how he went on to Rochester and "there saw the Cathedrall, which is now fitting for use, and the organ then a-tuning." The church must have been in a very bad state, for the dean and chapter reported to the bishop, in 1662, that the repairs that they had already executed had cost them £8,000, and that the defects still remaining in the fabric would need a further expenditure of not less than £5,000 to make them good. They said that they were unable to raise this sum themselves, but they remitted a quarter of the arrears due to them towards it. The under steward, Sir Henry Selby, gave up his salary for as long as should be thought fit; and several donations are recorded in the minute books, with the donors' names.

At this time Mr. Peter Stowell paved with freestone a great part of the body of the church, from the west door to the choir steps, at a cost of £100. This had been rendered necessary, probably, by the saw-pits mentioned above. He also recovered at his own expense the iron frame for the pulpit hour glass, and got back many books, records, etc., belonging to the church that were in the custody of Mr. Duke, of Aylesford. Under the Commonwealth, Stowell had for his loyalty suffered fine and imprisonment. He was joint registrar to the bishops from 1629 until his death in 1671, and was buried in the cathedral.

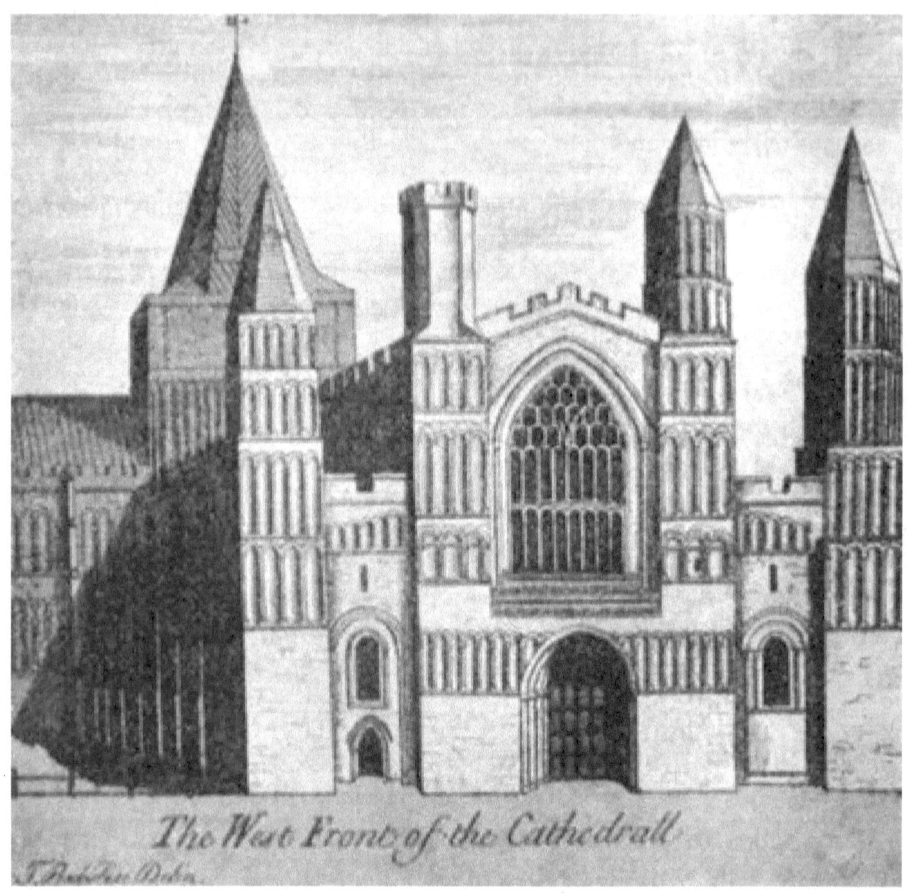

NORTH-WEST VIEW, EARLY EIGHTEENTH CENTURY

(From An Engraving Published In 1719).

In 1664 the south aisle of the nave was re-cased, and in 1670 an agreement was made with Robert Cable, to take down a length of 40 feet of the north aisle wall and re-erect it from the ground.

During the reign of King Charles II. two remarkable funerals took place in the cathedral. The earlier of these was that of Cossuma Albertus, Prince of Transylvania, who, having been driven out by the Germans, came to Charles II. for succour. He is said to have been kindly received and given a sufficient maintenance. This prince was approaching Rochester on the 15th of October, 1661, when his chariot stuck fast in the mire within a mile of Strood, probably at Gad's Hill ("that woody and high old robbing hill," as our Norwich officer called it). He resolved to sleep in his coach, and was there killed, with his own hanger, and plundered by his coachman, Isaac Jacob, alias Jacques, a Jew, and his footman Casimirus Kausagi. The murderers were afterwards caught in London, and executed, the footman having confessed. Cossuma's body was found on the 19th. One arm was brought by a dog to its master, a doctor of physic of Rochester, who was out for a walk near, and a search was then instituted. Two contemporary accounts of his death and of his funeral, which took place on Tuesday, the 22nd, have been found. From one of these, in the "Mercurius Publicus" of October, 1661, the following is taken: "His body being brought to the parish of Strood was accompanied from thence to the west door of the Cathedral Church of Rochester by the Prebendaries of the said church in their formalities, with the gentry and commonalty of the said City and places adjacent, with torches before them. Near the Cathedral they were met by the choir who sung Te Deum before them; when Divine service was ended, the Choir went before the body to the grave (which was made in the body of the Church) singing Nunc dimittis. Thousands of people flockt to this Cathedral, amongst whom many gave large commendations of the Dean and Chapter, who bestowed so honourable an interment on a stranger at their own proper cost and charges." The exact site of this grave cannot be pointed out. An account of the other funeral is to be seen in the diary of John Evelyn for 1672. We there read: "June 2, Trinity Sonday, I pass'd at Rochester; and on the 5th, there was buried in the Cathedral Monsr Rabinière, Reare Admiral of the French squadron, a gallant person, who died of the wounds he received in the fight. This ceremonie lay on me, which I perform'd with all the decency I could, inviting the Mayor and Aldermen to come in their formalities; Sir Jonas Atkins was there with his guards, and the Deane and Prebendaries; one of his countrymen pronouncing a funeral oration at the brink of his grave, which I caus'd to be dug in the quire." Such was the funeral of a brave ally; the English and French were then fighting together against the Dutch.[9] It is interesting to note here that the corner of his coffin, in a position such as Evelyn describes, beneath the choir, was touched when the tunnel was being made, in Sir G. Scott's time, to connect the organ with its bellows in the crypt.

The steeple, a little later, had much attention devoted to it. It was in a dangerous way in 1679, and Mr. Guy, a celebrated architect, was asked to report on it. He stated that it was very ruinous and ready to break down into the church; that the plates were rotten, the girders quite rotted through, and all the lead so thin that it could not be repaired; that three corners also of the stonework were so rent and crooked that they would need to be taken down. "He supposed that the making good of the stone tower, the taking down of the old spire and putting up of a new, and to sufficiently cover the same with lead would cost £1,000 over and besides the old lead and timber." His was a very alarming statement, but he was not intrusted with the superintendence of this extensive piece of work. The dean and chapter seem to have hoped that the matter was not really quite so serious. A few months later they consulted Henry Fry, a carpenter of Westminster, and he declared that the mending of the lead and of one end of a beam at the lower end of the east side of the spire would be sufficient to keep it from falling. He was evidently skilful

[9] A longer account of the funeral was published in the Gazette at the time. Its date is given as the 6th May in the Cathedral Registers, but this must be wrong.

and honest, for with his, and some slight subsequent repairs, the spire stood for another sixty-nine years. One would think that he deserved more than the 30s. paid to him for his visit and report.

A sum of £160 was, in 1688, spent on the repairing of the old organ and on a new chair organ, a name often wrongly altered to 'choir organ.' In 1705 the nave was newly leaded, the names of Henry Turner, carpenter, Thomas Barker, plumber, and John Gamball, bricklayer, being inscribed with those of the bishop, dean, prebendaries, and verger on one of the sheets. The altar-piece of Norway oak, "plain and neat," which retained its place throughout the century, was probably constructed in 1707. A sketch of its history, with notices of the various adornments that it had at different times, will be given when the furniture of the choir is described. In 1724 a return was made to Bishop Bradford that three-quarters of the whole roof had been re-leaded within the previous twenty years, and that the rest was believed to be in good order. There was then no defect in the walls reported; the windows were said to be in good repair and the pavement also. Until 1730 the bells were rung from a loft or gallery over the steps to the choir, the approach being from Gundulf's tower. This gallery was then removed, and the vaulting of the crossing finished to match that of the south transept, which had been repaired and decorated not long before according to a plan by Mr. James. At the same time the order was given for the part of the organ screen towards the nave to be wainscoted.

Very considerable repairs and alterations were made in the choir during the years 1742-43, under the direction of Mr. Sloane. While they were in progress, for the space of a year and a quarter, the dean and chapter attended service at St. Nicholas Church. New stalls and pews were erected and the partition walls wainscoted; a pavement was laid "with Bremen and Portland stone beautifully disposed;" and an episcopal throne was presented by Bishop Wilcocks and placed opposite the pulpit, where the present throne now stands. Much white-washing was done at this time, even the numerous Purbeck marble shafts being covered with it. In 1788, however, they are mentioned as polished once more and restored to their original beauty. From shortly after the Restoration until about the time of these alterations, the inclosure of the bishop's consistory court had been situated near the west end of the south aisle of the nave. It was now removed to the Lady Chapel, where it remained until well on in the present century.

The steeple had, at last, to be rebuilt in 1749. Mr. Sloane's model of its woodwork was for many years preserved in St. William's Chapel, and has since been kept in the crypt, where it still remains, but in a very dilapidated condition. In 1763 the northern of the towers flanking the west front was considered to be in a dangerous state, and was taken down, together with the upper part of the north aisle end beside it. It was rebuilt soon afterwards. A bequest of £100, in 1765, by Dr. John Newcome, dean of the cathedral and master of St. John's College, Cambridge, towards the repair of the fabric, was probably intended to help this work. The new tower was professedly a careful reproduction of the old, but its incongruities have formed one of the reasons for the recent thorough renovation, instead of mere repairing, of the west front. It was only carried up to about half its former height, and was there, with the aisle end, finished off with battlements. This was all done before 1772, as an engraved view of the west front in that year shows. The southern tower is in this view still unlowered, but it was cut down, to match its fellow in height, soon afterwards.

For a long time previously the outer walls of the south choir aisle and south choir transept had occasioned great anxiety. They were not buttressed originally, like the similarly situated walls on the other side of the church, probably because they had the cloister and other conventual buildings to support and shelter them. Several attempts were made, in particular, to render the transept secure. A first was by the fixing of wooden ties, with large iron bolts, in the main timbers of the roof; a second, in 1751, in pursuance of advice by Mr. Sloane, by the raising of two great brick buttresses; and a third, about twenty years later, by lightening the roof. These were useful for a time, but, as the wall was still evidently declining, Mr. Mylne was consulted and, by his direction, piles of bricks were erected in the undercroft, and other methods were used to discharge the weight of the upper works. These schemes were brutal and inartistic. Though they answered their purpose for some years, they were afterwards found to be doing harm rather than good.

In his "History of Kent" (1782) Hasted gives expression to some very gloomy views as to the state of the fabric. We there read: "The whole bears venerable marks of its antiquity, but time has so far impaired the strength of the materials with which it is built, that, in all likelihood, the care and attention of the present chapter, towards the support of it, will not be sufficient to prevent the fall of great part of it, even in their time." Dr. Denne, however, thought the case, though bad, not quite so hopeless as this, and his more sanguine opinion has proved to be correct. Constant care, however, has had to be bestowed on the place.

A fine new organ was constructed for the cathedral in 1791. During the closing years of the eighteenth century or the earliest ones of the nineteenth occurred the destruction of the upper portion of Gundulf's tower, which was, before it suffered this injury, one of the most curious and interesting pieces of architecture in England. Some sketch-books of Mr. Essex, who was, in the closing years of last century, employed on restorations in the cathedral, are preserved in the Department of MSS. at the British Museum. They contain many notes on, and sketches of, the building and details in it, but nothing of interest for this history as they do not illustrate his work in the church.

NORTH-WEST VIEW, EARLY NINETEENTH CENTURY

(From An Engraving By John Coney, 1816).

Since the close of the Napoleonic wars the cathedral has passed through four busy periods of restoration. The first of these lasted from the beginning of 1825 until about 1830. Mr. L. N. Cottingham was in charge, Messrs. Bayfere, Smirke, Savage, and Twopeny being also consulted at various times. The roofs of the choir and its transept, though they had been thoroughly repaired only fourteen years before, were soon found to be quite unsafe and so eaten up with dry-rot, that it was necessary to renew them. The part of the south wall between the main transept and the chapter room was also dangerously out of the perpendicular. The great masses of brick within and triangular buttresses without, the clumsy attempts of the eighteenth-century architects to save it, had by their subsidence even increased the mischief. Cottingham removed them and built up the wall, which deviated twenty-two inches from the upright, with a face of ashlar which constituted an invisible buttress. He also found that the central tower consisted to a great extent of rubble, and was incapable of supporting the spire. He almost entirely rebuilt it from the roof, and left it in its present form, finished with corner pinnacles but without a spire. All these serious works affecting the safety of the fabric involved the setting aside, to a great extent, of restoration in an ornamental sense. The east end was, however, considerably improved by the removal of the huge altar screen that concealed much of it. He opened out and renewed the lower range of windows there, of which the central had been quite, and side ones partially, blocked with brick, and lowered the altar and its pavement, to show the bases of the chancel pillars. The ugly upper window he merely restored, and left it for Sir G. Scott to erect in its stead the more appropriate tier of lancets that now take its place. Cottingham also renewed many other windows, including the great west one, those on either side of the presbytery, and the Decorated one by the chapter room. In the nave some red brick flooring had York pavement substituted for it, and in the choir some Grecian panelling and a cornice along the side walls were removed. The stalls also were repaired, and the paint cleared off the seats in the choir. There are two other pieces of work in connection with which Cottingham's name is often mentioned. One of these was the restoration of the chapter house door, with parts of which much fault has been found. The other was not so remarkable in itself as for a great discovery that it led to. I refer to the removal, quite at the beginning of 1825, of the mass of masonry that had long concealed from view the famous monument of Bishop John de Sheppey, whose effigy was made almost perfect by the careful re-fitting of some fragments that were found. Unfortunately Cottingham had it re-coloured, though the fact seems generally forgotten.

Various other faults in Cottingham's work have since been pointed out, but at the time his restoration received much praise. On the 30th of November, 1827, we find the dean and chapter voting him an honorarium of £100, as a token of their appreciation of the ability and zeal that he had shown.

The opening years of the fourth decade of the century form our next period, during which Cottingham still had the direction of the works. He now substituted the present rich and elaborate, but not altogether praiseworthy roof of the main crossing, for the plainer one that he had placed there earlier, when he rebuilt the tower. He restored the canopy of Bishop John de Sheppey's monument, designed a new pulpit, and a new bishop's throne for the choir, and later, in 1848, was responsible for a new font in the nave. These will be described and their several fates recorded later.

To Mr. Cottingham we also owe a repair of the ceilings of the choir and nave, and a final cleaning from whitewash of the Purbeck marble shafts throughout the building. He cleared the crypt out thoroughly, lowered the ground there to the base of the columns, repaired the whole, and, especially, renewed the shafts. The organ was enlarged by Hill in 1842, at Canon Griffith's expense; and at that of his wife, in 1852, the Lady Chapel was restored.

From the year 1871 till his death in 1877 the fabric was entrusted to Sir G. Scott, and the work in it was all carried out from his designs and under his immediate superintendence. At an early stage of his work he put the clerestory of the nave in sound repair, and the western arm of the church was then used for services while the restoration of the choir was in progress. During the latter part of the time its aisle walls were underpinned. To the western transepts and crossing Scott devoted much attention, considering rightly that they formed one of the most elegant parts of the structure. He largely repaired the masonry of both the south and north transepts, underpinned the former's end, inserted some new windows in the west wall of the latter, and gave it a new doorway and massive oak door, in place of the ruinous entry that before existed. He did away with the low eighteenth century roofs and gables of both, restored the former gables, chiefly on the authority of old prints, and erected roofs of the old high pitch once more. In the south transept he made good, also, the interesting vaulting, with its oak ribs, which were decayed and threatening to fall. The spaces between them, which had been formerly boarded, he found filled only with lath and plaster. To the organ screen he gave back its original plainness, which made it rather an eyesore, as there was now no further screen in front of it, on the other side of the transept, as there had been when St. Nicholas' altar stood at the east end of the nave. For the organ a new case was made after his design, which, without any removal of the instrument or parts of it, preserves the vista of the choir. In making a tunnel to connect the organ with its bellows in the crypt, many interesting discoveries were made.

We now come to Sir G. Scott's work in the choir; it was very thorough. He restored the gables to the east end, the north transept, and the aisle of the latter, but had not funds to raise the roof to correspond. At the same time he replaced where they had been lost the curious little pinnacles that surmount the flanking turrets of the north choir transept and of the east end. The ugly, upper east window he, after some hesitation, decided to do away with, though it was in sound condition after Cottingham's repairs. In its place was erected the present group of lancets, which are certainly more appropriate, and have, with the tier below, from which he removed some inserted decorated tracery, a very pleasing effect. The high altar was removed from the east end to its old position, some distance in front, with a free passage all round. For this old situation conclusive evidence was found when the floor of the presbytery was lowered to show the bases of the piers round it. For the altar Scott himself designed its new reredos, and the greater part of the eastern arm was floored by him with encaustic tiles, though some would have preferred a pavement less showy and glittering in effect. The designs of most of these tiles were taken from a few old ones still to be seen in the choir transepts. Under his direction, too, new stalls for the dean and prebendaries were erected under the organ, and new stalls for the choir constructed. In these latter as much earlier work as possible was preserved. On the wall above them he restored a painting of which he found considerable portions still remaining there. He also designed the new pulpit, which was put in a different position to that of its predecessor, and the new throne. The earlier pulpit, by Cottingham, was removed to the nave, and the old throne went later to St. Albans. By far the greater part of the money for the work of all these three periods was found by the dean and chapter themselves, and for this they deserve great praise. The new choir furniture was, however, provided for by Dr. Griffith, — who had been formerly canon here, — and his wife, with a donation of £3,000. Earlier instances of their liberality on the building's behalf have been already given. The episcopal throne was the gift of Lord Dudley; and Dr. Claughton, then bishop of the see, gave the brass lectern in the choir.

A little later the rather plain stalls in the nave were erected by the Rev. A. Cazenove, an honorary canon, in memory of his father, who died in 1880. After the death of the late Dean Scott, the great lexicographer, it was decided to raise a memorial to him in his cathedral. The memorial took the form of a decoration of the choir screen with a series of statues under canopies. This was designed by Mr. J. L. Pearson, and, though not faultless, is a great improvement on the plain, flat wall left by Sir G. Scott.

Mr. Pearson has also been intrusted with the direction and superintendence of the last great restoration, which has been devoted chiefly to the famous west front. After its underpinning in 1888 a thorough repair of it was undertaken. This was absolutely necessary, for, in many places, the facing was leaving the core, and, in some, pieces of it had already fallen. Many of the stones needed replacing; in all such cases careful copies were substituted one by one. The great west doorway was thoroughly restored, its shafts were given separate bases once more, and new doors took the place of the old. The works, of this period also, were carried as far as possible by the dean and chapter, but on the 27th of October, 1892, an influential meeting was held at the Mansion House to find funds for their continuance. Subsequently the north flanking tower — in its then form, the work of the eighteenth century — was demolished, and entirely rebuilt for the second time, both it and its fellow being now raised again to their original height. A comparison with the illustration given on p. 26 of the front as it was in 1719, shows how careful and accurate the restoration has been. The north aisle end was at the same time restored to its old form, and the northern gable turret, — a curious specimen of fifteenth century work, which many were sorry to see disappear, — replaced by a copy of its fellow on the south.

After the death of Canon Burrows, in 1892, the new font, just within the west door, was erected by subscription, as a memorial to him.

The last piece of work that we have to record is the inclosure of a series of new vestries along the south side of the crypt. These have been paid for "with American dollars," the proceeds of Dean Hole's recent lecturing tour on the other side of the Atlantic.

THE CATHEDRAL FROM THE CASTLE GARDENS

(From A Photograph By F. G. M. Beaumont).

The cathedral still has great and pressing needs. The most crying is, perhaps, the fitting of roofs to Sir G. Scott's gables in the eastern part, for their present isolated condition makes them unpleasantly conspicuous. This the dean is anxious to see undertaken next. A spire is also much wanted; the present tower, especially since it has been dwarfed by the raising of the transept roofs, looks scarcely worthy of a moderately important parish church, much less of a cathedral. However, when it is found possible to undertake the change, it should be remembered that

Rochester is a small cathedral, and that the opposite fault to the present insignificance must also be avoided. The new spire must neither be too lofty nor too elaborate. Finally, as Sir Gilbert Scott pointed out, the parapets of the nave and its aisles are unworthy of the building, and a considerable amount of internal repair is necessary. These matters will have to be seen to as soon as the requisite funds can be found.

CHAPTER II.

THE EXTERIOR, MONASTIC BUILDINGS, ENCLO-SURE, AND GATES.

Rochester lies within a bend of the Medway and is bounded by that river on the north and west. It is girt round by chalk hills, which, on the two sides mentioned, look down on it from across the stream. Its houses have now begun to climb the hills in greater numbers, but the space that used to be enclosed by the old city walls lies very low, the only piece of rising ground within their line being the mound on which the castle stands. The cathedral church is one of the smallest in England, and occupies a lowly position immediately beneath this mound and the mighty keep that crowns it. It can claim attention therefore neither by magnitude and grandeur nor by prominence of position. Its tower is, however, next to the castle keep, the most conspicuous object in the town, and this fact makes our regret the greater, that it is not more worthy of its position.

The cathedral, though unable to bear comparison in the matter of size with most others, and though by no means an imposing building, is a very interesting structure and well worthy of all the study and care bestowed upon it. It bears in itself many marks of its eventful history, and the work of finding these and solving their significance is a most attractive one. Many of its features, too, are important architecturally. The crypt, the Norman work in the nave, the great west doorway, and that leading to the chapter-room, all rank among the best examples of their respective kinds in England.

An excellent bird's-eye view of the cathedral can be obtained from the castle, either from the keep itself, or from a convenient opening in the outer wall. On the church's own level good views can be obtained of almost all the principal parts, though in some directions buildings interfere. The famous west front can be well studied from the road before it; and from a favourable position on the other side of the old cemetery, a good north-west prospect can be obtained. Passengers along the High Street are now, by the substitution of an iron railing for a former wall, enabled to gaze on the north side of the choir and the ruins of Gundulf's tower, across a stretch of turf that generally bears visible testimony to Dean Hole's love of flowers. A general view of the whole south side, together with the few remains of the monastic buildings, can be obtained from the road through the precinct; and, of the exterior of the building, the east end alone cannot be well seen except from private ground. There are other, more distant, views, which are both interesting and picturesque.

TOWER AND BELLS

The Central Tower is the first feature to claim our attention now that we are come to the description of the exterior and its parts. The earliest tower over the crossing was raised, in 1343, by Bishop Hamo de Hythe, who crowned it with a spire of wood, covered with lead, and placed in it four bells, named Dunstan, Paulinus, Ythamar, and Lanfranc. This spire and the masonry of the tower caused great anxiety at the end of the seventeenth century, but with some not very considerable repairs then, and some slight ones later, lasted until 1749. Its height was 156 feet, but the authorities for its form do not at all agree. It is given a very uncommon shape in the north prospect by Daniel King, reproduced on p. 14. This seems to be followed by many engravings which, however, bring no additional testimony, for they do not correct great faults in other parts of it, such as the insertion of a bay too many in the nave, and the ignoring of a story in the transept ends. The north-west view from Harris's "History of Kent" (1719) makes the spire octagonal, and it appears of this form in many small sketches. Other engravings, as another view in Harris's own book, show it square, but without the peculiar treatment of the middle of each side, and with something simpler and plainer than the pairs of dormer windows in the plate by King. Some reasons may, however, be given for thinking the latter's version of the spire correct, though his engraving is elsewhere so inaccurate. Such are: (1) its abundant detail, perhaps too abundant, as others do not support his dormer windows, for instance; (2) the fact that Browne Willis, in his "Mitred Abbies," refers to this "draught" (when used to illustrate Dugdale's "Monasticon"), in preference to attempting a description himself; and (3) that the tiny view shown on the portrait engraving of Dr. Thorpe that forms the frontispiece to his "Registrum Roffense," agrees with it well when we take into consideration the smallness of its scale. The tower was square, without either battlements or corner pinnacles, and the spire rose directly from it. On the west side, it will be noticed, the blind arcading under a string course at the height of the ridges of the transept roofs, terminated downwards on the lines of a pointed gable, and we may hence conclude that the nave used to have a high-pitched roof before its present flat one.

The spire raised in 1749 was octagonal, and rose directly from the tower. It had neither parapet nor corner pinnacles to hide the transition from the square to the octagon, nor splaying to make this change less abrupt. Its form is shown in the 1816 view (p. 31), and Mr. Sloane's model of its woodwork is still to be seen in the crypt, in a very damaged state. A curious instance of the inaccuracy of some old engravings occurs in two plates by Metcalf, and by Ryland after B. Ralphe, which reproduce the same view of this cathedral, and are, apparently, only variations of the same plate. They represent the tower itself as octagonal, make it of excessive breadth, and give it three windows in each face.

The new spire was demolished, after an existence of a little less than eighty years, by Mr. Cottingham, who took down at the same time most of the old tower, and raised the present rather plain one, which bears no spire. Our illustrations render any description of the form of this tower unnecessary. It did not meet with approval, even before it was made more insignificant in appearance by Sir Gilbert Scott's heightening of the transept roofs. An apologist for Mr. Cottingham says that he was not altogether responsible for its faults, since he was compelled to modify his design, through a strong conviction among the townspeople, especially among the local builders, that he was overloading the supporting piers. He obtained expert opinion that they were capable of bearing twice the weight, but at last yielded, though he complained that by his so doing his work was spoiled.

NORTH-EAST VIEW, WITH RUINS OF GUNDULF'S TOWER

(From A Photograph By Messrs. Carl Norman And Co.).

The Bells are hung in this tower. They are six in number, and their sizes range from 34 to 52 inches. Mr. Stahlschmidt, from whose "Church Bells of Kent" the following particulars are derived, regrets that he could find nothing of the bell-history of the cathedral between 1343, the date of Bishop Hamo's four, whose names have just been given, and 1635, the year in which the present third bell was, according to its inscription, made by John Wilner. In 1683 Christopher Hodson, a London founder, re-cast the fifth and tenor bells for £120. The contract, which describes him as of St. Mary Cray, where he had probably a branch establishment, still exists, and he seems to have done the work near by, perhaps even within the precincts. The treble was re-cast by John Wood, of Chancery Lane, in 1695, at a cost of £9, and the contract for this work also is still preserved. In 1711 Richard Phelps, a well-known founder, supplied an estimate for the re-casting of a cracked bell (the fourth) weighing 15 cwt. He did not, apparently, obtain the commission, for this particular bell is recorded to have been re-cast during the next year by James Bagley, of Cripplegate, London, on behalf of his father Matthew, who was then near the end of his career. After finishing this work James, on his own and his father's behalf, warranted the bell sound, and, further, that the second, which he agreed to turn, "the striking sides being much worn," should be "as good as a new bell and retain the same note." This, the second, bell is the only one that bears no inscription; the fifth has, besides its inscription, the royal arms on its waist. The treble was again re-cast by Pack and Chapman, of London, in 1770, and in 1834 the tenor was re-made by Thomas Mears. After all these re-castings, it would be interesting to know how much old metal, from Bishop Hamo's or even older bells, the present peal still contains. Mention will be made of some very early bells when Gundulf's tower is described.

WEST FRONT

The West Front has recently been very carefully restored. Its great central window, and the flat gable above, belong to the Perpendicular period, but all the rest is either original Norman work, or as accurate a reproduction of this as possible.

In design the façade surpasses those of many cathedrals. The aisle ends, for instance, are not here, as in some cases, carried as screens to a greater height than is structurally necessary. This is more correct and, at the same time, allows the flanking towers to be more imposing and effective.

The nave end, the main central portion of the front, contains the great west door, to be described later, and over it the great window, inserted during the second half of the fifteenth century. The dripstone of the window terminates in two carved heads. On each side of the doorway is a round-headed recess, and on the level of the door-arch, and interrupted by it, runs a row of blind arcading, the shafts of which rise from plinths, that project in carved heads from an elaborate string course. The first complete bays of this arcade, on the north and south sides of the door, contain niches, within which statues of two bishops, Gundulf and John of Canterbury, were placed, in 1894, by the Freemasons of Kent. These statues are not at all worthy of praise. The space between the heads of the arcade and the decorated string course, crossing at the level of the window sill, is filled with a diaper pattern. There are three more blind arcades above, all interrupted by the window, before we come to those that run round the gable turrets. The lowest has a band of chevron moulding crossing the tops of its shafts, while carvings fill the lunettes in its heads. Next come two rows of a double interlacing fret, and then another string course, from which the second row of arcading springs. This has semicircular heads, with zigzag ornament, and a double series of intersecting arches above, like an arcade on Anselm's Tower at Canterbury. The topmost arcade of the three rises over another string course and is round-headed like the rest. Its arches do not, however, like theirs, run on continuously but form two groups of two on each side. The crenellated gable parapet rises from a string course with five sculptured masks, and has plain shields on its battlements. Of the gable turrets the northern has, in the last restoration, been made to match the southern. Both are now octagonal, and have two arcaded stories. Their tops are pyramidal, and ribs run down the edges from the curious conical cap, which crowns the apex of each.

The aisle ends stand back somewhat. Each has a lofty, ornamented arch, rising to the height of the sill of the central window, and containing, recessed within its upper part, a semicircular headed window. We see, higher up on each side, a single narrow light, and higher still an arcaded lean-to. At the end of the north aisle is a pointed doorway, inserted for the use of St. Nicholas' parishioners in 1327.

We will now conclude our account of the front in its present form, with a description of its flanking towers. The northern is square for its whole height, and has four rows, one above the other, of blind arcading. The southern, with the same number of arcades, is also square in its lower portion, but, for the two upper rows becomes octagonal, and finally terminates in an octagonal pyramid. The spire of its fellow on the north can scarcely be called octagonal; it is square, with the angles only slightly cut down, and with slight splaying at its base. On the summits of both are curious conical caps (like those described as surmounting the gable turrets), from which ribs run down the angles. The arcades are continued round the outer sides of the lower parts of the towers, and right round when the roofs of the aisles are passed. The heads of all the arches are as usual semicircular, and the second arcade from the top is filled with a diaper of semicircles arranged in a curious scale-like pattern.

Generally, as we have said, except for the great Perpendicular window and the gable above it, the front shows the design of the later Norman builders. The window that they constructed in it was possibly wheel-shaped, but we have no representation of the cathedral previous to its supplanting. The parts of the front that show their old form now have not, however, all continuously retained it. At the time of the erection of the Perpendicular clerestory to the nave, the northern gable turret was rebuilt in the curiously plain, octagonal, flat-topped form, which the oldest engravings of the front illustrate. It has only quite recently been altered again to the earlier shape of its fellow on the south; and is the only feature in which there is any conspicuous difference between the front as now seen and as shown in our early eighteenth century view. An earlier, seventeenth-century view exists, in which, if it were not so inaccurate, the front would have the same appearance. In this, however, as in his north prospect, Daniel King shows his great liability to err. We can point to the insertion of one tier of arcading too many in the central portion of the front, and to the omission of the windows at the ends of the aisles, as well as of the small door.

Our next view of the front dates from 1816, and shows the form in which it was left by the great changes of 1763 and the succeeding years, when the northern flanking tower, having been found to be in a dangerous state, was quite taken down. Its rebuilding (up to only half its former height) and that of the upper part of the adjoining north aisle end, was completed before 1772 at any rate, and was professedly as accurate a reproduction as possible of the older work. It was finished off with battlements. A comparison makes manifest other changes besides that in the height. The first arcade was at a lower level; in the aisle end the narrow light disappeared; and the old lean-to was replaced by a blind arcade of three arches, the central higher than the others. A little later the south-western tower was correspondingly lowered, but no further changes were made in it, and soon afterwards a precinct gateway that used to stand against it was cleared away.

CAPS OF WEST DOOR, NORTH SIDE

(From A Photograph By H. Dan).

The front then remained untouched until 1888, when underpinning was undertaken preparatory to a thorough restoration. After much of the older work had been carefully repaired—in some places renewed stone by stone—an attempt was made to undo all the work of the eighteenth century architects. All that they had erected was taken down and rebuilt, and all that they had demolished, as accurately as possible replaced. The work was carried out under the direction of Mr. J. L. Pearson, and for the skill and care shown in it, he has deserved, and receives, much praise. It is regretted however by many that he did not preserve the north gable turret as he found it, since it was so curious a specimen of fifteenth century restoration. One may hope too that smoke and weather will soon tone down the new masonry so that it may be in less glaring contrast with the old.

CAPS OF WEST DOOR, SOUTH SIDE

(From A Photograph By H. Dan).

WEST DOORWAY

The great West Doorway, like the rest of the original work remaining in the front, dates from later Norman times,—the first half of the twelfth century. It is formed by five receding arches, and every stone of each of these is carved with varying ornamental designs. Between the second and third of them runs a line of cable moulding, an ornament which occurs also inside the door. Each arch has its own shaft, and the groups of five on each side are elaborately banded. The shafts have richly sculptured capitals, and in those on the south side, as well as in the tympanum, the signs of the Evangelists appear. The shafts second from the door on either side are carved with statues, two of the oldest in England. These are much mutilated, but they were thought worthy of great praise by Flaxman. That on the spectator's left is said to represent King Henry I., and the other his wife, the "good Queen Maud." This attribution is probably correct, as these sovereigns were both great benefactors to the cathedral, and were living when the front was being built. The figure of the queen has suffered the more; it is recorded to have been especially ill-used by the Parliamentarians in the days of the great Civil War. The tympanum contains a figure of Our Lord, seated in Glory, within an aureole supported by two angels. His right hand is raised in benediction, and his left hand holds a book. Outside the aureole are the symbols of the four Evangelists: the Angel of St. Matthew and the Eagle of St. John one on each side above the Winged Lion of St. Mark and the Ox of St. Luke similarly placed below. A straight band of masonry crosses beneath the lunette, and has carved on it twelve figures, now much mutilated, but supposed to have represented the twelve Apostles. All the sculptured work of the portal has suffered greatly from age and exposure and from the hand of man. In the recent restoration the coping has been renewed, the shafts have been given separate bases once more, and many of the most worn stones have been replaced by new ones carved in facsimile. Mr. Clifford's beautiful drawing of the doorway (facing p. 3) is especially valuable as he was able to take exact measurements of all its parts while the repairers' scaffolding was still standing. The doors that he pictures have since been replaced by a more elaborate pair with richly scrolled hinges and strengthening bands of iron.

This entrance is one of the best known features of the cathedral, so it will be interesting to quote the words of a few great authorities concerning it. Fergusson, speaking of the cathedral in his "Illustrated Handbook of Architecture," says: "Its western doorway, which remains intact, is a fair specimen of the rich mode of decoration so prevalent in that age. It must be considered rather as a continental than as an English example. Had it been executed by native artists we should not entirely miss the billet moulding which was so favourite a mode of decoration with all the nations of the north." Kugler, the great art historian, also thinks it continental in style, and compares it with the architecture of the south-west of France. We even find it spoken of, on account of the richness of its ornamentation, as Saracenic in character. The late Prof. Freeman, in his "History of Architecture," is liberal with his praise, and probably all Roffensians, at any rate, will agree with him, when, in speaking of Norman doors with tympana, he says: "the superb western portal at Rochester Cathedral is by far the finest example of this kind, if not the finest of all Norman doorways."

The doorway is structurally interesting, as we have therein exemplified a curious mode of forming a straight head over an aperture. The arches of course bear all the weight of the super-structure, but the straight band of masonry on which the figures of the Apostles are carved has to support both itself and the stonework of the tympanum. The method by which it is enabled to do this is as follows: the stones, the joints being vertical, are locked into one another by semicircular ridges fitting into corresponding indentations. Mr. Smirke, writing on aperture heads in "Archæologia," vol. xxvii., said that he thought these excrescences, or in masons' language, "joggles," insufficient for security, and suggested that perhaps inside, out of sight, the joints radiate like those of a skeme arch. He also commented on the irregularity of the stones used here and throughout the whole front. Another fact worthy of remark is that the semicircular arches of the doorway are struck from slightly different centres.

The Mayor and Corporation of Rochester still have the right of entry in their robes and with their insignia of office by the great west door. We find the privilege of having their insignia borne in the cathedral on record as early as 1448 in indentures between Bishop Lowe on the one part, and the bailiff and townspeople of Rochester on the other. The titles "mayor" and "citizens" were only granted later by Edward IV., in a charter dated December 14th, 1461. In the indentures it was agreed, among other matters, that the bailiff and his successors might cause to be carried, before him and them by their sergeants, their mace or maces—and the sword likewise if the king should ever give them one—not only to and in the parish church, but also in the cathedral and cemetery, especially on festival days, and processions, and solemn sermons, and at the reception and installation of bishops, and at all other fit times. On the other side they were to make no execution or arrest within the precinct of the monastery and the palace of the bishop, except the same should be specially required of the bishop or prior whenever the same was made. Similar rights were granted to the dignitaries of other cities about this time. For instance, in 1447 they were conceded at Exeter, and at Worcester in 1462. A sword did not become a part of the Rochester insignia until quite recently, after the castle had been acquired as the property of the city. One, given by Alderman J. R. Foord in 1871, is now worn by the mayor as its constable. Besides the sword the insignia include a great mace, two sergeant's maces, a silver oar (in token of admiralty jurisdiction over the Medway), two constable's, and eight borsholder's staves, besides the mayor's chain and badge.

Pepys, speaking of the visit to the cathedral of himself and some friends in 1661, tells, in his diary, that they went "then away thence, observing the great doors of the church, as they say, covered with the skins of Danes." He is so accurate an observer that this must be taken as conclusive evidence that there was such a tradition in his time, and some ground for it, though no other record of anything of the kind is to be found. However, even if it were likely, which many people will deny, that the skins of Danes were ever nailed to church doors at Rochester, it certainly is not that they would have been transferred by Normans from the Saxon cathedral to their new one, or that, if so transferred, they would have survived the fires and other dangers through which this afterwards passed. There are traditions of the existence of human skin on doors at Worcester Cathedral, where it is said to have belonged to a robber who stole the sanctus bell from the high altar, and at Hadstock and Copford, East Anglian churches. In these latter cases the Danes are again mentioned. In 1848 all these doors had been removed from their original positions (the old north doors of Worcester being still preserved in the crypt) but Mr. Way succeeded in obtaining fragments of the parchment-like substance from each for microscopic examination. They were declared to be, in each case, human in their origin, and to have belonged probably to fair-haired persons. These cases show flaying not to have been unknown in England, even, to judge by the Worcester case, after the Norman Conquest, and confirm the passages in records that seem to refer to its existence.

NAVE AND MAIN TRANSEPT

The Nave has nothing else remarkable in its exterior. The perpendicular windows in the north aisle wall, part of which was rebuilt in 1670, are two-lighted, with irregular quatrefoils in their heads. Those of the southern aisle, which was re-cased in 1664, are single-light, and only three in number, — in the second, third, and fourth bays from the west.

The insertion of Perpendicular windows in the aisles took place about the middle of the fifteenth century. The plainness of the south side, where the Lady Chapel does not hide it, is perhaps explained by the fact that it used to be hidden by the Cathedral Almonry. The westernmost bay of each aisle is plain, and the next on the north side contains the now walled-up Perpendicular doorway, inserted, when their new church was built, for the entry, in their solemn processions, of the parishioners of St. Nicholas, who passed out again by the west door. It is contained within a rectangular framework, and has quatrefoils in the spandrels.

In the corner between the south aisle and the transept is the Perpendicular **Lady Chapel**, three bays long from east to west, and two in width towards the south. Its windows are three-lighted. They terminate in the obtuse arches of their time and have their heads filled with tracery. At about half its height each is divided by a transom or horizontal mullion, beneath which the lights have cusped heads. The chapel was originally vaulted, so is well buttressed, which the aisle walls are not. The north aisle wall has its bays marked by flat pilaster-like buttresses, and the southern has still less support, for the similar buttresses rise only to the original level of the ground, which is now cut away for a few feet along the side of the church.

The North Transept is in the Early English style. Flat buttresses with offsets halve the sides and flank the end. The high gable, with three circular windows and flanking pinnacles, is the work of Sir G. Scott, who rebuilt it, in place of the low, commonplace one that had replaced it about seventy years before. He also raised the roof to its original pitch. The occurrence of blind arches between the windows here is to be noticed, making continuous arcades of which the heads are carried by single shafts. The windows in the northern bay of the west wall were all inserted by Scott, who found only dilapidated blind arcades there, and the doorway in its present form is also by him, he having found the old entry very ruinous. The east side used to be almost entirely hidden by Gundulf's tower, and is still slightly concealed. It has therefore no windows except in the clerestory, and some bays even of this have none.

The South Transept is of rather later date than its fellow, and belongs to the Early Decorated period. Its very interesting gable was lowered, with the roof, at the same time as that of the north transept, but has fortunately, like it, been replaced by Sir G. Scott. The chief authority for the restoration seems to have been an engraving in the 1788 edition of the "Custumale Roffense." The gable stands back a little and has its base hidden by a parapet rising above a decorated string course. Beneath a sculptured bust, near the apex, is a chequer-work cross, and lower still a band of chequer-work bearing three shields of arms, the dark squares in each case being formed by flints. The central shield contains the arms of the see, that on the left three crowns, and that on the right a cross with martlets. The transept is well buttressed, and the gable is flanked by pinnacles, beneath which curious gargoyles project. The five graduated windows of the upper range have double shafts on each side, and the connected dripstone over the lower range ends in carved heads. The clerestory of the west wall looking out over the aisle and Lady Chapel roofs is similar to that on the east side and the quatrefoil heads of the two-light windows help to mark the entry into the Decorated period. The little room in the angle between the transept and the choir aisle is used as a vestry and will have to be mentioned again.

CHOIR AND GUNDULF'S TOWER

The North Side of the Choir can, as has been said, be well seen from the High Street. To one or two points in it attention may well be drawn. In the window heads, the dog-tooth moulding, the characteristic ornament of the Early English style, constantly occurs, and the openings often have side shafts. In the lower tier of the presbytery windows Decorated tracery has been inserted; elsewhere we have Early English work, or, frequently, a modern copy of it. The lowest row of windows lights the crypt. The gable at the end of the north choir transept, that above the east wall of its aisle and that at the east end of the church, are all by Sir G. Scott; they still require roofs of corresponding pitch, a need both great and conspicuous. The gables replaced by these present ones were flat and late in period. The east end and the transept end are both flanked by towers, with double gables crowned by curious little pinnacles, copied by Scott from one still remaining. The east gable has three graduated windows, that to the transept aisle a quatrefoil within a dog-toothed circle. The present form of the east end is altogether due to Sir G. Scott; and to it and its history we shall devote more attention in describing the interior of the church. This part of the fabric is well buttressed.

Of **Gundulf's Tower**, on the north side of the choir, between the main and choir transepts, only ruins now remain, but these are older than any other part of the church's buildings still in existence above ground. The tower was certainly Gundulf's work and built before his church. The construction of the latter rendered useless two out of the four long narrow windows that had been inserted in the tower, one in each side, on the ground floor, and they were therefore blocked up. The tower, though rather dilapidated, was still almost complete at nearly the end of the last century. A view in Grose's "Antiquities," vol. iii., shows it as it was in 1781. At that time it still rose as high as the parts of the church beside it, and traces are to be seen in the print of the flying bridge that formerly connected it with the Early English turret at the north-west corner of the choir transept. There is now, however, only a mere shell of the lower part left. The walls were 6 feet thick, inclosing a space 24 feet square. In the "History and Antiquities of Rochester" (1772), we are told that there were at that time traces of one floor at a height of 20 feet, and of another 25 feet above that. The walls then rose 20 feet more, giving a total height of 65 feet. During the Early English period the north-east angle, which stands quite clear of the church, was strengthened by massive buttresses, and a story, apparently of wood, was added on projecting arches resembling machicolations. This wooden story probably formed the bell chamber; the machicolation-like supports still existed in 1781.

There has been much discussion as to the original purpose of the tower. Some leading antiquaries of the eighteenth, and of the early part of this century, thought that the bridge entrance at the top was at first the only one and that the structure with its massive walls formed the cathedral treasury. It must be remembered, however, that the early English turret to which the bridge was thrown was not in existence until much later. The lower part still remaining is so dilapidated, with all its ashlar facing gone, that it seems impossible to fix the position of the original entrance. At the present day there are two entrances, one through a large opening in the north wall, the other through a doorway in the south-west corner formed by knocking out the back of an old recess.

It seems very likely that the tower was primarily intended to be a defensive work. Whatever its original purpose, however, it is certain that it was used for bells at a very early date. In or before 1154, for he died in that year, Prior Reginald "made two bells and placed them in the greater tower. One which was broken was applied to the making of another bell." In support of the view that the tower was a defensive work the suggestion has been made that the metal thus re-used may have belonged to the original alarm bell. Two other bells came to the cathedral in the twelfth century, and were probably placed here at once as they are mentioned in the "Custumale Roffense," written about 1300, as then hanging in the "greater tower," a name by which this is distinguished from the long destroyed south one. Gundulf's Tower is certainly, therefore, an early example of a detached campanile, and, if built as such, was probably the first in this country.

As has been before mentioned, its reduction to a mere ruin is of quite recent date. The author of the 1772 edition of the "History and Antiquities of Rochester," thinking it a bell tower, wrote in that work: "May the present reverend and learned gentlemen (the Dean and Chapter), and their successors, experience the necessity of finishing this venerable tower and applying it to the uses for which, it has been conjectured, it was originally intended." In the second edition, of 1817, stands: "So far, we regret to say, is this ardent wish from having been realized, that a part of this ancient tower has lately been taken down to supply materials for the repairs of the church." Denunciations follow of the action of the dean and chapter in thus demolishing one of the most curious and interesting pieces of architecture remaining in England.

The space between the tower and the church seems to have been floored and occupied by the wax-chandler's chamber and the sacristan's rooms. The remains of an oven and chimney, conjectured to have been used for the baking of altar-breads, have also been described.

The South Side of the Choir presents no very remarkable features. A brief history of the efforts to save it during the latter part of last century, and in 1825 and the following years, has been given in our opening chapter. The wall of the choir aisle is supported by a flying buttress as well as by the small room in the corner between it and the south main transept. In the wall are three lancet windows, the easternmost with dog-tooth ornament, and a fine doorway, which used to open into the western range of the cloisters. The ends of the outer mouldings of the doorway arch, which also have the dog-tooth, bend round and upwards in an unusual way that is worthy of notice. All that can be seen of the transept end is by Cottingham. He gave it a new ashlar facing, which, as the wall was considerably out of the perpendicular, constituted an invisible buttress. His destruction of the old brick buttresses was a great improvement. The same architect found no gable, and built the present rather flat one containing a circle ornamented with zigzag mouldings. In the south wall of the transept aisle is a Decorated window with beautiful tracery. This window was of course an insertion. Remains of recesses on each side of it, like those still in the transept end, made this evident until 1825, when they were hidden beneath the smooth modern surface. The southern wall of the presbytery is almost entirely concealed by the eighteenth century chapter room, with its plain, square-headed, sashed windows. The clerestory, however, which is like that on the north side, appears over the red-tiled roof of that modern structure. In the basement on this side some windows have quite recently been inserted, to light the new vestries in the crypt, and a door opens into the cellar beneath the chapter room.

MONASTIC BUILDINGS

The Monastic Buildings and Cloisters originally stood in the usual position on the south side of the nave, and were apparently of wood, but these first structures having soon perished, their successors were erected in an uncommon position, said to be unique in this country, on the same side of the choir. At Lincoln, also, the cloister is indeed beside the the choir, but to the north of it. The earliest monastic buildings at Rochester were of Gundulf's time; the next, in the new situation, were the work of Ernulf, who built the chapter house, dormitory, and refectory. Of these fine specimens of later Norman architecture, ruins still exist. The chapter house and dormitory formed the east side of the cloisters. Of the western wall of the chapter house three arches remain, with a recess, having zigzag mouldings continued down to its base, and not merely round the head, on each side of the central arch, between it and the others. The chapter house was an oblong room, as some remains of it within the deanery prove, and must have been fine and of ample size. It was raised above the ground level, and the space beneath, into which the three lower archways (now walled up) opened, was looked upon as an honourable place of burial; it was entered by the middle arch, the side shafts of which have fine and elaborate capitals, while the arch itself is richly sculptured and has elaborate zigzag and other mouldings. The panels round it are said to contain representations of the twelve signs of the zodiac, but all the carved work here (general in Caen stone) is so worn and decayed that it is impossible, in most cases, to feel sure of what was intended. The damaged state of all the carved work is possibly to some extent a result of the great fires of the twelfth century. Ernulf's diaper occurs in the spandrels on either side of this central arch; and each of the outer arches has zigzag and billet mouldings and, within them, a row of a diaper pattern. Passing on to the south the next arch also has zigzag and circular mouldings, while its lunette is occupied by a relief, now so worn that the subject is scarcely discernible. It represents Abraham's sacrifice of Isaac. The father holds his son with his outstretched left hand, and is about to slay him, when God's hand appears in the clouds above. Behind Isaac is seen the ram that was afterwards to be offered in his stead, and in the opposite corner, behind Abraham, there seem to be traces of two small figures, probably the two servants who had been left at a distance to await the patriarch's return. This interpretation is confirmed by three words of an inscription, which still remain round the inner part of the arch (*Aries per cornua*). Beneath the lunette runs a fine band of foliated ornament, including birds. The capitals are rich, and an angel and a bird appear in those on the south side. Continuing southwards the still remaining lower portion of the dormitory west wall has a blind arcade with double intersecting heads, semicircular like all the other arches here, but interrupted once or twice by an uncut arch.

NEW CHAPTER ROOM AND RUINS OF THE OLD

(From A Photograph By J. L. Allen).

On the south side of the cloisters was the refectory; the lower part of its massive north wall still remains, and in it a fine doorway, with a groined lavatory and towel recess, the work of Prior Helias about 1215. The great thickness of the wall is, as will be explained shortly, probably due to the fact that it was originally a part of the old fortifications of the city on this side. The cellarer's and other storerooms were, apparently, on the west side, and there seems to have been a smaller guesten-hall to the south-east. Some corbels that helped to support the cloister roofs are still to be seen, projecting from the south wall of the church, and from Ernulf's buildings. The doorway opening from the church into the western range has been already described. Of this range itself nothing remains, but at its southern end there is yet to be seen, half buried, a late Perpendicular porch. This stands beside the road between the north main transept and the Prior's Gate, and opens towards the episcopal precinct.

RUINS OF CLOISTERS, EAST RANGE

(From A Photograph By H. Dan).

BISHOP'S PALACE

Of the old **Episcopal Palace**, famous for having been the home, during his later years, of Cardinal Fisher, a considerable part still exists to the south-west of the cathedral, between it and Boley Hill. The palace was perhaps originally erected by Gundulf himself. It is said to have been rebuilt, after a fire, by Bishop Gilbert de Glanvill (1185-1215), though he may have found it sufficient to repair the shell then left, using Caen stone for the purpose. Another definite notice of the palace is found when we see Bishop Lowe, in 1459, dating an instrument from his "new palace at Rochester." Here, again, it is probably a re-modelling and not a complete reconstruction that is referred to, but the re-modelling was certainly thorough, for many fifteenth century features are to be seen in the part that is left.

The main framework of the whole rectangular structure probably dates from Gundulf's or, at the latest, from Bishop Ralph's time; the simple plan and the walls, 3 feet in thickness, being such as might be expected in early Norman work. The building, which has a total length of 70 feet, is of stone, with a tiled roof, and now forms dwelling-houses. It has a massive buttress in the centre of the southern face, and the outlines of old windows can be traced in various parts. The western gable end, which can be seen from Boley Hill, is also interesting and worthy of attention. The cellars and vaulted passages extend even beyond the building to the eastward, and are very massive in their construction. Fragments of wrought masonry that probably once belonged to the chapel have been dug up; they were mostly portions of capitals, with beautiful foliated ornaments, or of column shafts.

Cardinal Fisher was the last Bishop of Rochester to reside here. He received a visit from Erasmus in 1516, and this great scholar gave a very bad account of the residence and its situation. Fisher himself complained of its dilapidated state and of the rats that infested it. Cardinal Wolsey stayed at the house with the bishop on the 4th of July, 1527, and wrote to the king on the next day: "I was right loveingly and kindely by him entertained." After his cook's attempt, in 1531, to poison him and his family at his London house, on Lambeth Marsh, Fisher stayed continuously at Rochester, until, in 1534, he was peremptorily summoned to the capital—never to return. The palace was continued to the bishops by the charter constituting the new establishment, but they neither inhabited it nor, in fact, lived much at Rochester at all. On the spot where its old prison used to stand within the palace precincts, the diocesan Register Office was erected in 1760.

The building at present known as the palace, in St. Margaret's Street, has often been thought to be the old mansion with all these historical associations; it did not, however, become the property of the bishops until after 1674. In that year it was bequeathed by Francis Head, Esq., to his wife, with the arrangement that, after her death, "in case the Church of England does continue so governed by Bishops of the true Protestant faith," it should be settled on the Lord Bishop of Rochester and his successors for the maintenance of hospitality near the cathedral church, and as an invitation to him to preach once a year each at the churches of St. Margaret and St. Nicholas in his cathedral city. This building has been little used by the bishops, and has generally been leased by them, like other residences of theirs, of which mention will be made in the chapter on the see and its history. The small episcopal revenue has usually only allowed of the maintenance of a single palace, though more may have been desired and even necessary.

ENCLOSURE AND GATES

The Enclosure and Gates of the cathedral and priory have an interesting history. The church was so close to the south wall of the city, which bounded its domains on that side, that we find the line of the fortifications moved time after time to allow of the growth of its dependencies. Three acres of land, as appears from a deed of quit-claim executed by Gundulf, had been acquired by the monks, about 1090, on the south side of the town, and fenced round by a wall, which was probably of slight construction, as no traces of it have been found. The first extension of the city walls, which at the Conquest still followed the old Roman lines, was made, also in Early Norman times, near the south gate, so as to enclose the episcopal precinct, within which the palace was then built. A little later Ernulf had to make more changes to obtain room for his new monastic buildings. For this purpose he too overstepped the old wall and used it apparently to form the northern side of his southern range which lay just beyond. This would explain the massiveness of the north wall of the refectory, which is 7 or 8 feet thick, while the other walls are only 2½ or 3 feet. In this old wall is the fine transitional doorway here pictured, with round arches, but with the well-known dog-tooth moulding. Its inner trefoil arch is of a form very uncommon in this country, but more usual on the Continent. Having gone beyond the old wall, Ernulf had to raise a new one; this ran from the south-east corner of the city to the corresponding corner of the bishop's precinct. He probably then erected a predecessor to the present Prior's Gate, for we find a gate of this name mentioned on the site, before the one now to be seen was erected.

ARCHWAY IN THE ROMAN WALL

(From A Photograph By H. Dan).

Ernulf's wall continued to be the boundary of the city until 1344, when there was again an extension to the south. To this time our present Prior's Gate probably belongs. The new wall, of which the demolition must have been complete in 1725, when Minor Canon Row was built on its line, was about 5½ feet thick, about 16 feet high, and crenellated. Its foundations have to a great extent been traced. Later—it is not certain at exactly what date—still more of the monastic property was enclosed by yet another wall, of which the course is to some extent known.

THE PRIOR'S GATE IN 1825

(Drawn By H. P. Clifford From A Lithograph By W. Dadson).

In 1344 we find measures taken for the first time to isolate the priory from the city. The erection of screens and doors guarding the approaches to the monastic part of the cathedral has been recorded, and we now read of the raising of a strong wall to the north of the church along the side of the High Street. This was possibly due to ill-feeling between the monks and the parishioners of St. Nicholas, possibly to dread of the bands of travellers, soldiers, and pilgrims passing through the town on their way to Canterbury or the Continent. It is to be observed, however, that other ecclesiastical precincts were similarly protected about this time. The close at Lincoln was walled round in Edward II.'s reign, as evil-doers resorted thither and made attendances at night services dangerous, and to the same period is assigned a like protection of the close at Salisbury. Edward I.'s patents authorizing these walls of 1344 are both printed in the "Registrum Roffense."

Gates to the Enclosure. The Prior's Gate, to the south of the main transept, has already been mentioned as dating from the middle of the fourteenth century. Our illustration shows it as it appeared in 1825; when it formed a portion of the Grammar School, of which more is to be seen in the building to the right. The upper story was afterwards used as the school-room of the chorister boys, but a new building has recently been erected for them. Entrance to the cemetery and to the west door of the cathedral was formerly, and can still be, obtained through the rather later College Gate, which stands beside the High Street, opposite the end of Pump Lane. This has also been known as Chertsey's or Cemetery Gate, and has been identified as the Jasper's Gateway of Edwin Drood. Earlier than either of the two just mentioned was St. William's Gate, which stood on the site of the Post Office, to the north of the main transept, to which it led from the High Street. It has now quite gone. Its constant use rendered a fourth, the Deanery Gate, necessary to keep private the priory grounds. This gate still existing, was formerly called Sextry or Sacristy Gate, and dates from Edward III.'s reign, being probably later than Prior's Gate though earlier than College Gate. Yet another gate was built at the southern end of the west front, because College Gate was always open to the parishioners of St. Nicholas. This porter's gate was in existence during the last century, but now both it and the cathedral almonry that used to stand near by have disappeared. The only other gate within the precincts, that at the south-west angle of the cloisters, has been already mentioned. College Gate and Deanery Gate now have upper stories of wood, which form parts of dwelling-houses.

EASTGATE HOUSE, ROCHESTER

(From A Drawing By R. J. Beale).

CHAPTER III.

THE INTERIOR.[10]

The cathedral church of Rochester is, as has been already said, a very small one, and we must not expect to find in it the grandeur and impressiveness that great size often confers. As a whole, too, it is not remarkable for beauty, though special parts may claim to possess this attribute. Its chief claim to attention is its excellence as an example of the gradual additions and successive alterations made to and in old buildings during the long periods of their existence. In different parts of the fabric specimens can be seen of almost all the noteworthy variations of style that appeared in English ecclesiastical architecture from the Early Norman to the Perpendicular period. Some opinion as to the merits or demerits of various restoring architects during the last three centuries may also be formed in it, for a very considerable amount of their work remains in evidence. Many features of the building are indeed remarkable in other respects, but we are probably correct in saying that, as a whole, it is, to students of architecture, chiefly historically interesting.

The Ground Plan is of the double cross form, frequent in buildings of this class. The nave and choir both have aisles, but those of the choir are walled off from it. The main transept is aisleless, but the north and south choir transepts have each an aisle, or small chapel, on the eastern side. Beneath the whole eastern part of the church extends the magnificent crypt. The total length of the building is 305½ feet, of which 147½ feet belong to the eastern arm. The main transept is 120 feet long, the choir transept 88 feet.

---

[10] The numbers in [] in this section refer to the plan.

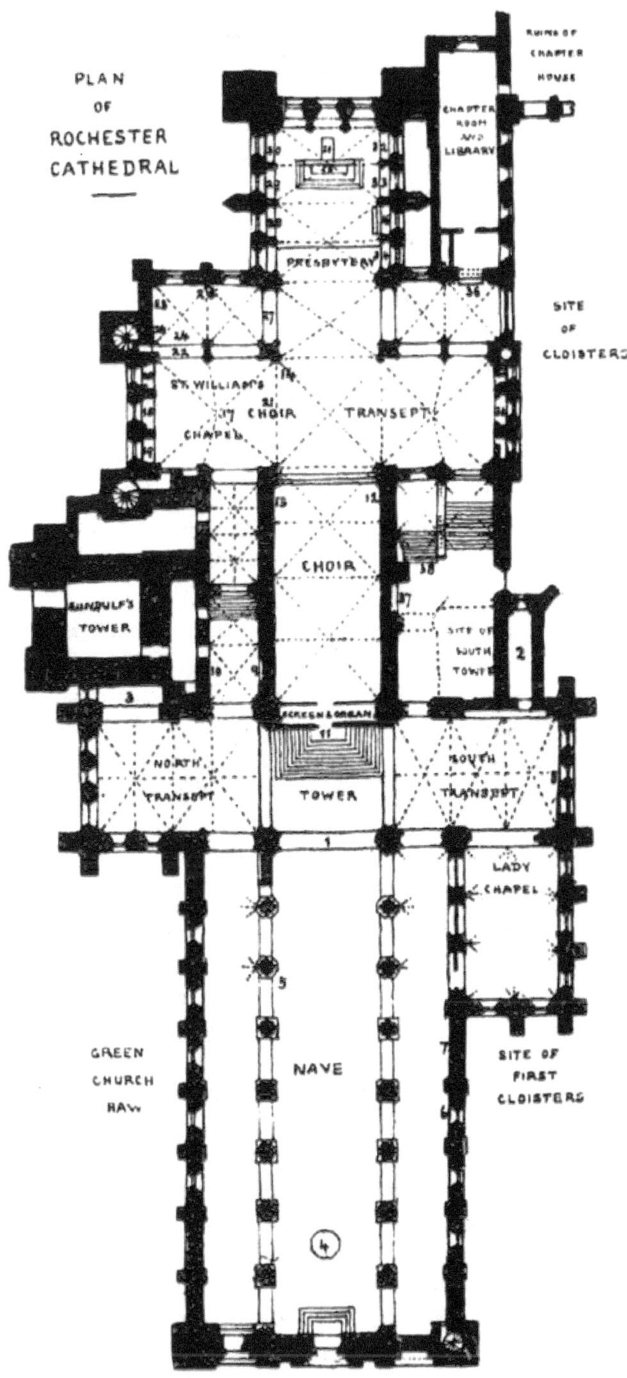

PLAN OF ROCHESTER CATHEDRAL

NAVE

The Nave.—After passing beneath the great west doorway, through its new richly-hinged doors, we descend by a flight of four steps into the nave. On the inner side of the doorway arch are found a fine cable moulding, occurring also on its outside, and the billet moulding, of which the omission is so noticeable there. In the blind arcades that decorate the nave end inside, we see, besides plain mouldings, specimens of both the zigzag and the billet. The two upper arcades are so abruptly cut by the great Perpendicular window as to make most conspicuous the fact that this is a later insertion.

Of the aisle ends the northern contains the early fourteenth century doorway, inserted for the use of the parishioners of St. Nicholas' altar, while the lower part of the southern has a blind arcade of three arches like those at the same level on either side of the great west door. Each aisle end has also a round-headed Norman window, with a plain circular moulding, and of the two small lights above, the northern belongs to the recent restoration. In the south-west corner of the nave is a beautiful little Norman doorway, which, opening into the tower flanking the front on that side, has a fine embattled moulding round its arch. The shafts of this small door, of the great west door, and of the aisle end windows, all have scalloped caps, and other caps of this form are seen in the arcades.

We will now, leaving the inside of the front, direct our attention to the nave arcades. Rochester and Peterborough possess probably the best examples of the Norman nave in this country, and the former is interesting, also, as possibly giving us some idea of the appearance of this part of the Norman church at Canterbury. The connection between the archiepiscopal cathedral and this its eldest daughter was always close, and the resemblances that can be pointed out in them are still numerous. Mr. Parker, by the way, was so struck by the similarities in later, Early English, work, as to suggest that the Rochester William de Hoo may have been the William the Englishman, the younger William, of Canterbury.

It has been noticed that the architecture is plainer here than in contemporary examples in France, but lighter, probably because intended to have a wooden roof. From the west wall the Norman work extends as far as the sixth bay of the nave arcades, the seventh and eighth bays being, with part of the sixth, the work of Early Decorated builders. The half piers at the west wall and the Norman piers facing each other in the nave arcades form pairs, but each pair differs from the rest. The pier capitals are flat, with scalloped ornaments. The semi-cylindrical shafts starting from them are now stopped by the plain string course that divides this from the next story. If they were continued further they would only emphasize the irregular placing of the Perpendicular clerestory windows, but they probably rose originally to bear the main timbers of the roof. The arches of the lowest story are semicircular, of course, and are in two orders. Both orders were, it is believed, plain throughout, in early Norman times, and they still continue to be so on the aisle side of the south arcade. The inner order is still plain everywhere, but the outer has zigzag and other mouldings. In each bay of the triforium, the tympanum is filled with an elaborate diaper around a central ornament. This decoration varies in every bay, and is thought to be a later insertion. It is noteworthy that the triforium arcades open into the aisles as well as into the nave, an unusual arrangement, which seems, however, here to be part of the design of the twelfth century. This opinion is supported by the existence of the narrow gallery, now blocked up, in the thickness of the wall. The early Norman triforium arcades seem to have been removed by the architects of the following period, and replaced in the present form. The aisles were perhaps originally vaulted; the flat pilasters of their outer walls might then have been built as vaulting shafts. If such was the case, the vaulting must have been found too heavy for the walls, and a wooden roof have been therefore adopted in its stead. The easternmost bay of the triforium, on each side, is apparently later Norman like the rest, but is really the work of masons of the Decorated period. It had been demolished in connection with the rebuilding of the nave, in progress at that time but abandoned when only two bays were finished. It was then found that the best way to make the junction of the styles good would be to restore the old work as accurately as possible. This was well done, but differences of material and in methods of working save us from being deceived.

The two bays of Early Decorated work, just alluded to, complete the nave eastwards. The transition from the round-arched to the pointed style is made still more conspicuous by an increase in the height of the arcades, which involved the discontinuance of the triforium; and the banded shafts of dark Purbeck marble clustered round the later piers also emphasize the change. The two piers at the junctions of the styles do not pair, but we cannot regret the difference on the south side, as we owe thereto the beautiful foliated capital here illustrated (p. 68).

The clerestory of the nave is divided from the stories below by an enriched string course. It is of the same style throughout and dates from the Perpendicular period. The predilection of the architects of that time to substitute work of their own for that of their predecessors in clerestories and great west windows of ecclesiastical buildings, has been noticed by many writers. At Rochester they could not in either case resist temptation. Their clerestory contains plain and uninteresting three-light windows, which are, moreover, unsymmetrically placed with regard to the arches beneath them. The roof is apparently of the same date; it is flat and of wood, carried by corbels carved and painted to represent angels bearing shields.

THE NAVE, LOOKING WEST

(From A Photograph By H. Dan).

The two tower piers at the end of the nave, where the latter joins the main transept, have their Purbeck marble shafts stopped at some height from the ground. The most likely explanation of this is, that there used to be here a solid stone screen

(1), or rood loft, against which the parish altar of St. Nicholas stood before 1423. On the west side of the northern of the two rises a mass of masonry, so high as to partly block the arch. It is built, to a great extent, at any rate, of old materials, for on both sides of it are to be seen stones with fragments of plaited Norman diapers. The purpose of this masonry has been the subject of much discussion. It was at one time generally believed to have been raised, as a buttress, to aid the pier in supporting the weight of the tower, but this notion has since been ridiculed. The tower, we are reminded, was not raised until 1343; the stability of its piers had been secured before this date by the two new bays of the nave, and additional support can not have been needed. Others suppose that the masonry belonged to the stone screen spoken of above. A fine walled up arch on the north side adds to rather than lessens our difficulties. It has good mouldings,—springing from the capitals of two Purbeck marble shafts, of which the eastern has unfortunately been broken away,—and the dripstone terminates in a head, so mutilated that the face is quite lost. This archway seems too wide to have been the entrance to the stairs leading to the rood loft, a use which has been suggested for it. The occurrence of the above-mentioned fragments of diapers on the wall within the arch, as well as on the other side of the mass, may perhaps justify us in concluding that these two surfaces are both of the same date, and that the archway was walled up originally.

CAPITAL, SOUTH ARCADE OF NAVE

(H. P. Clifford Del.).

It seems possible that we have, after all, a buttress to deal with here. It is known that the north transept and the north-west tower pier were raised before the adjoining parts to the south and west, but many have supposed that the north tower-arch was not thrown across until later. If it was built at the earlier time, a temporary support to the pier against its thrust may have been judged expedient, until the new work at the end of the nave should be completed. The mass that we are discussing seems to have been hurriedly raised with old materials at hand, and, from the carelessness which allowed fragments of old ornament to appear here and there on the surface, not to have been intended to be permanent. It was not until 1320, or later, apparently, that the design of rebuilding the nave was finally abandoned, and a junction of the new and the Norman work made. It seems, therefore, no great thing to suppose that the originally temporary support lingered on until 1327, to be then retained in connection with the oratory made, *in angulo navis*, for the Reserved Sacrament, for the parishioners of St. Nicholas. I have never seen or heard of any record as to which corner is the *angulum* referred to. It is known, however, that provision for the reservation of the Blessed Sacrament was often made to the north of the altar, and that we find Sacrament Houses in this position in churches that possess them.

The Aisle Walls have the bays marked by flat pilasters, to be traced back perhaps to Early Norman vaulting shafts. Springings of the Early Decorated vaulting, that once covered the two eastern bays, are still to be seen, but the aisles are now roofed with wood throughout. String courses are continued beneath the windows, which latter have been described and commented on in our chapter on the exterior of the church.

Lady Chapel

The so-called **Lady Chapel** was really built as a nave to the Lady Chapel proper in the south transept. On the east side a single broad arch opens into the transept, and in the wall above are to be seen traces of the outer mouldings of the two arches (like those on the north side) that this single wide one replaced. A tablet on the south wall records that the chapel was restored, in 1852, by M. E. G., *i.e.*, the wife of Canon Griffith. It is now used for morning prayers by the Grammar School, and for some sparsely-attended services. From 1742 until well into the present century the Bishop's consistory court sat here, after having been held formerly at the western end of the south aisle of the nave. The chapel seems to have been vaulted, and we have, perhaps, to regret here the loss of a fine fan-traceried roof.

The South Transept is of the Early Decorated period, and rather later than its fellow. In the east wall, opposite the wide arch leading into the so-called Lady Chapel, two bays were, about 1320, included under one arch to form a larger recess for the altar of the Blessed Virgin Mary. The king and queen corbel heads of this arch were once painted, and the colours are said to have been still tolerably fresh in 1840. The clerestory windows on each side are two-lighted, with quatrefoil heads. They have a gallery running before them, but the screens to this vary. On the east side the screen before each window has a broad pointed arch of the width of the window, flanked by a pair of narrow ones; on the west it copies the window. The occurrence of the dog-tooth moulding should be noticed. The transept end has an upper range of five single-light pointed windows, graduated in height towards the centre, divided by narrow blind arches, and having a screen arcade of five arches in front, one arch before each light. The whole arrangement of the end is shown in our illustration. Figures in fresco could, in 1840, in spite of coats of whitewash, still be traced on the lower part of the wall.

THE NAVE, LOOKING EAST

(From A Photograph By H. Dan).

BAY OF NORMAN WORK IN NAVE

(From A Drawing By H. P. Clifford).

The roof of the transept is almost entirely of wood, though in the form of a quadripartite stone vault with longitudinal and transverse ridge pieces. The springings of the ribs are indeed of stone but otherwise the ceiling is of wood throughout. Sir G. Scott found the whole greatly in need of repair, — the ribs rotten and decayed, and the spaces between them filled principally with plaster, — and thoroughly restored it.

This part of the church, and all the rest to the east of the nave, is enriched with shafts of the famous dark marble from the quarries of the Isle of Purbeck. The vaulting shafts of this material are generally carried to the ground, but over the head of the wide outer arches in the east and west walls here, they rise from finely carved console heads.

At the southern end of the great altar recess in the east wall, a small pointed doorway opens into the little room (2), so noticeable outside, in the angle between the transept and the south choir aisle. This room, like so many other parts of the building, has had considerable vicissitudes. Here are said to have been kept at one time the valuables belonging to the altars in this part of the church. Then, at the end of the eighteenth and during the earlier part of this century, the room is mentioned and marked on plans as the coal hole. It is now more honourably used again, as the vestry of the masters and king's scholars of the Grammar School, who have to attend the cathedral services on Sundays and Saints' Days.

Main Transept

The Crossing is noticeable for the finely clustered shafts — the tower piers. The clearance hence, in 1730, of a ringers gallery has been already mentioned. In 1825 Mr. Cottingham found the space vaulted. His changes in the tower included a re-placing of the vault with a flat wooden ceiling, of which the main beams ran from east to west. This he changed again in 1840 for the present more elaborate, but not altogether satisfactory ceiling, with its great cross beams and pendant bosses. An admiring contemporary account tells us that the largest of these bosses, though looking so small from below, are 3 feet 3 inches in diameter, while the beam mouldings are 5 feet 3 inches in girth, and the wall mouldings 5 feet 7½ inches. The ceiling is coloured, but for neither colouring nor ornament does it deserve praise.

The North Transept was erected about 1235, in the Early English period and style. The screens to the gallery before the clerestory lancets have a main arch in each bay, with dog-tooth moulding, divided into three by Purbeck marble shafts placed the width of the window apart. In each bay without a window there is a row of blind arcading, which, like the mouldings of the arches by which the gallery passes through the wall piers, springs from carved corbel heads. In the transept end the screens before the three lancets of the clerestory are of the usual form, but are adapted to their graduated heights, and there are small additional arches, one at each side.

THE NAVE FROM THE NORTH TRANSEPT

(From A Drawing By R. J. Beale).

The arch opening into the north aisle shows a curious device for preserving a different level on each of its sides. On the transept side we see the mouldings of an arch like, and on the same level as, its neighbours to the north. The western half of the whole thickness of the wall is, however, continued lower, exhibiting a plain surface to the east, but terminating on the aisle side, at the height of the eastern arches of the nave, in mouldings that we should have expected to find higher up. This lower level was necessary on account of the vaulting at this end of the aisle, of which traces still remain, but the whole arrangement was clumsy, and we cannot be surprised at not finding it repeated on the other side of the church.

THE SOUTH TRANSEPT

(From A Photograph By H. Dan).

The next bay has on the triforium level a curious windowless recess, the mouldings of whose arch spring from two shafts on each side. There is another very similar recess opposite, but with only single side shafts.

The two northern bays of the east wall are occupied by a wide and deep recess (3), the arched ceiling of which rises to within 3 or 4 feet of the clerestory level. The outside shafts, and those from which the central ribs of the ceiling used to spring, have all gone, though their caps remain. Within this great recess there is, on the spectator's right, a small one, with side shafts, containing a piscina. On the left, in the church's north wall, is a window, which rises to only half the height of the pointed arch, with side shafts, within which it is inclosed. It was at one time the general belief that this recess used to be the site of the parochial altar of St. Nicholas, which may possibly have stood here during the short time between the completion of the north transept and that of the new work at the east end of the nave, for a document published in the "Registrum Roffense" tells us that, after a dispute about a removal, the position before the pulpitum was assigned to it in 1322. Arrangements were then made to avoid any mutual disturbance of the services of the monks and the parishioners, and the new church for the latter was already talked of. The writer of the "History and Antiquities of Rochester,"[11] quotes a will that suggests a possibility that an altar of Jesu stood on this spot.

The transept end and its west wall have windows of the same form at the triforium level, and there is a similar resemblance in the blind arcades below, except for the doorway restored by Sir G. Scott, and surmounted by an obtuse arch. The arch to the east of this doorway was cleared of masonry in 1840. A large figure, in distemper, of St. Christopher bearing the Infant Christ was then uncovered, but only to fall away as the air was admitted to it. Miss Stevens, daughter of the dean, made as complete a copy of it as possible, as stone by stone was carefully removed to disclose only a small piece at a time, and her drawing, with a note by Mr. Spence, is preserved in the British Museum.

The vaulting of this transept is rather remarkable. It is octopartite in plan, developed from the sexpartite form by the addition of a longitudinal ridge-rib which divides its larger cells. The fine bosses in both transepts merit attention, and so do the corbel-heads to the intermediate vaulting shafts in this one.

Font, Pulpit, and Stalls

The Font (4) standing in the centre of the nave, only a short distance from the west door was erected in memory of the late Canon Burrows, who held a stall here from 1881 until his death in 1892. Executed for the subscribers, in Hopton Wood stone, by Mr. T. Earp, it is round in form, supported by a central column, of quatrefoil section, and four shafts placed corner-wise, rising from a double plinth, on which, facing the door, is the brass inscription tablet. Round the bowl are four groups in relief, facing the cardinal points, with eight single figures inserted in pairs between them. The subject of the west group is "Suffer little children to come unto me;" then passing round to our left we see, in order, figures of Noah and

[11] Anonymous, but probably by the Rev. S. Denne and W. Shrubsole. Published in 1772; second edition, 1817.

Moses, the Baptism of the Gentile (typified by the Ethiopian), figures of St. Bartholomew and St. Mary Magdalene, the Baptism of our Lord, figures of St. Barnabas and St. Cornelius, the Baptism of the Jew (typified by St. Paul), and finally, figures of St. Lydia and St. Winfred.

The old font, now removed to Deptford parish church, used to stand beneath the second arch, from the west, of the south nave arcade. Made in 1848, this was first used in 1850. In form, it was square and enriched, and borne by a circular column and four corner shafts. A still earlier font is to be seen in an engraving made by John Coney during the second decade of the present century. This stood under the eastern side of the third arch of the same nave arcade, was octagonal in form, with panelled sides, and had a substantial railing round it.

The Pulpit (5) in the nave is more elaborate in form and decoration than that now in the choir. It was designed for the choir by Mr. Cottingham, in 1840, and stood there, opposite the bishop's throne, until it was removed to its present position by Sir Gilbert Scott. **The Stalls** are modern and very plain. A tablet on them tells us that they were erected in memory of Mr. Philip Cazenove, who died in 1880, by his son Arthur, an honorary canon. **The Lectern** is of carved wood, of the well-known form in which the book is borne by an eagle's out-spread wings.

Monuments and Slabs

Monuments.—The nave and main transept possess none that are very old or very remarkable, but the following seem to deserve mention. Against the south wall, in the fourth bay from the west, is the monument of John, Lord Henniker (6), who died in 1803. Over the sarcophagus in relief Honour is crowning Benevolence, while a medallion of the deceased, with a coronet and an unfolded patent of peerage, and his coat of arms are seen against the base. This monument was erected by J. Bacon, jun., in 1806, and is signed with his name.

The next bay to the east contains no window, but is occupied by the monument to Lady Henniker (7), who died in 1792, before her husband was ennobled. This monument is, to a great extent, constructed of "Coad's artificial stone," and rises beneath "a neat Gothic arch" of that material. It shows, on a base of gray marble, a sarcophagus of white marble between two figures of Time and Eternity. In this case the sarcophagus is detached and not in relief, and the figures also stand free.

On the wall at the end of the south transept, under the central window, is a monument to Richard Watts, Esq. (8), erected in his memory by the mayor and citizens in 1736. A coloured bust, with long gray beard, stands forth curiously above the inscription. This bust was given, to be placed here, by Joseph Brooke, Esq., whose family had acquired possession of Watts's house by purchase. There has been much discussion as to its material, which seems, however, to be not terra-cotta or some other composition, but firestone. Watts sat as member for Rochester in Queen Elizabeth's second Parliament, and we have already told how he had the honour of entertaining her 1573, at his house, "Satis." He is famous for the provisions that he made in his will for the relief of the poor of Rochester, Watts's Almshouses on the Maidstone road being one of the sights of the town; but he is perhaps best known of all for his foundation of the "House of the 6 poor travellers." Poor wayfarers, to this number nightly, "not being Rogues or Proctors," are here provided with supper, bed and breakfast, and presented besides with 4*d.* each when they leave. Wonderful tales of wicked lawyers have at times been current in explanation of this coupling of Proctors with Rogues, but the true explanation is that Proctor is used in a quite obsolete sense here. It has the same meaning, probably, as in the following passage from Harrison's "Description of Britain," 1577: "Among Roges and idle persons we finde to be comprised all Proctors that go up and down with counterfeit licences, cosiners, and such as go about the countrey using unlawful games," etc. It was used also of mendicant lepers, the "Proctors to some spittal house," and of men who carried dispensations about the country. Watts's will was proved on the 20th of September, 1579.

Just beneath the Watts monument is a brass tablet in memory of the writer who has made the House of the six poor travellers so well known throughout the English-speaking world. This tablet was placed here by the executors of Charles Dickens "to connect his memory with the scenes in which his earliest and latest years were passed, and with the associations of Rochester Cathedral and its neighbourhood which extended over all his life."

The same transept contains on its east wall a monument, with a medallion bust, to another charitable Roffensian, Sir Richard Head, an alderman of the city after the Restoration, and one of its members of Parliament in 1667. He was again member in 1678-79, and before this had been made a baronet. It was at his house that King James II. stayed, at Rochester, after his flight from London. Sir Richard died on the 18th of September, 1689, at the age of eighty, arranging by his will that the profits of some cottages and land at Higham should be distributed, to the amount of two shillings a week, in bread, to the poor at St. Nicholas Church. The overplus was at the end of the year to be divided among four of the most ancient men, and four of the most ancient women of the parish. The charity still remains, but its scheme has been to some extent modified by the Charity Commissioners.

In the same transept, near the entrance to the south choir aisle, stands a bust of Dr. Franklin, who died in 1833. This monument is by S. Joseph, and near it on the south wall is a tablet, with a medallion bust, in memory of Joseph Maas, the great tenor singer, whose name is not yet forgotten in the musical world.

The recess on the east side of the north transept contains a mural tablet in memory of Dr. Augustine Caesar, who died in 1683. This is chiefly remarkable for its pompous Latin inscription, which tells how he came, saw, and conquered diseases invincible to others, and calls on fevers and all human ills to exult now that their great foe has passed away in a happy death, and is as a Caesar, enrolled among the gods. From other sources we learn how he obtained his degree of M.D. from Oxford, in 1660, after a petition in which he explained that it was to escape oaths contrary to his loyalty, that he had forborne to take it during "the late troubles."

The Pavement of this part of the church is of plain stone. In the floor are still to be seen many **Memorial slabs**, but more have been either covered up or lost. In the centre of the south transept there still remains the matrix of what was once a splendid brass, representing a bishop, in his episcopal robes and with his crozier, beneath a rich canopy with a shield of arms on either side of his head. In the great recess in the north transept there is placed against the wall, lozenge-wise, the matrix of a brass of several figures. We are told, by Mr. Spence, of the existence, as recently as 1840, of three matrices in the south aisle, six in the nave, one in the north aisle, nine in the north transept, besides a tenth on the wall, and five in the south transept. Of the six in the nave, one near the steps at the west end had evidently held a fine episcopal brass, and another very ancient, had once contained the figure of a knight. There was also here a slab with a hollow, said to have been a socket for an axe, but evidently due to a wearing of the stone, a piece of Sussex marble. The death of Cardinal Fisher was said to have been commemorated by this. The specimen in the north aisle was very elaborate, intended for the figure of a bishop, in whose dress it was noticeable that both peaks of the mitre were intended to be shown. The matrix that Mr. Spence especially described in the south transept is evidently the one that still remains there. Besides all these matrices or sockets of brasses he mentions a slab to the north of the steps leading to the choir which he thought to be, probably, a coffin-lid reversed.

Stained Glass

The Stained Glass in the western part of the church is all modern. In it we see specimens of the work of Messrs. Clayton and Bell, whose later windows are certainly finer than their earlier ones. Even with their best before us we cannot, however, help wishing for old work. We hope to see soon all the clerestory and aisle windows bright with colour. They will then be more beautiful in themselves, and they will also moderate the glaring light which detracts much from the effect of the nave.

The great west window is, below the springing of its arch, separated into eight lights, which are divided into two tiers by a transom or horizontal mullion. Beginning from the left or south side we have, in the eight spaces of the lower tier, Abraham, blessed by Melchisedec after his victory over the five kings; Moses and the overthrow of the Egyptians in the Red Sea; Joshua commanding the sun to stand still; Gideon, overthrowing the Midianites; Jephthah's victorious return; Samson carrying off the gates of Gaza; David slaying the lion; and finally Nehemiah at the building of the walls of Jerusalem. In the upper eight spaces are single figures of the heroes celebrated in these scenes. In the next row, of twelve complete spaces, the lowest in the head of the window are the figures of other heroes. These are, in order, from the left, Caleb, Othniel, Deborah, Barak, Samuel, Jonathan, Beraiah, Jehosophat, Hezekiah, Josiah, Matthias, and Judas Maccabeus. Next above come ten military saints: SS. Maurice, David, Edmund, Alban, George, Andrew, Louis, Martin, Patrick and Gereon. There are besides in the head of the window devices of the corps of Royal Engineers; the badges of the grenade and crown; the national emblems of the rose, thistle, shamrock and leek; emblematic subjects, such as the Helmet of Salvation and the Breastplate of Righteousness; and armed angels. The arrangement of the window is well seen in our view of the nave looking west. It is in memory of the officers and men of the Royal Engineers who fell in the South African and Afghan campaigns. Their names are recorded in crudely coloured mosaic tablets in the upper of the two arcades below.

The window at the end of the north aisle is in memory of Lieut. T. Rue Henn, R.E., killed at Maiwand in 1880. It contains three medallions, of scenes from the life of Jonathan:[12] his victorious onslaught on the Philistines, made when attended only by his armour-bearer; his bestowal of his robes and arms on David; and his death, slain by the Philistines in the battle of Mount Gilboa.

The corresponding window at the end of the south aisle is in memory of Col. A. W. Durnford, R.E., who fell at Isandlwhana in 1879. This has three similar medallions illustrating great deeds of Judas Maccabeus:[13] his taking of the spoils of the "great host out of Samaria," with the sword of Apolonius their general; his exhortation of the small part of his army that had not fled to die manfully; and finally his death in this his last battle.

The only window with stained glass in the aisle walls is the first from the west on the south side, in memory of Lieut. R. da Costa Porta, who died in the Egyptian expedition of 1882. It has two scenes: Peter walking on the water, and Christ stilling the tempest.

The windows in the north transept end are filled with stained glass in memory of Archdeacon King. In the lower tier of three, we see, beginning from the left, a figure of St. Philip, the deacon, with a representation below of the laying on of hands (Acts, vi. 6); the Lord Jesus, with three angels on either side, and underneath a scene with six figures, including a saint in chains before a judge; St. Stephen, the proto-martyr, with the scene of his death beneath. Some money remained after the completion of these windows, so the upper range was also filled. In it are figures of the three archangels: St. Raphael, St. Michael slaying the dragon, and St. Gabriel.

The upper range of five windows in the south transept end commemorates the officers of the corps of Royal Engineers, who died in the Peninsular and Waterloo campaigns. Their names are recorded in the mosaic tablets in the lowest arcade at the west end of the nave. The subjects, from the left, are St. Maurice, St. Nicholas, St. George, St. James and St. Adrian. The three central of these windows have small scenes beneath the figures. The lower windows, given by the same corps, are in memory of General Gordon and others of its members who died in the Egyptian campaign. The three windows are each two-lighted, and each light contains a single figure. There are represented in them, in order, St. Florian, St. Gereon, St. Martin, St. Alban, St. Denis, and St. Longinus. The Royal Engineers, it will be seen, have appropriately chosen Old Testament heroes, and military saints for representation in all their glass.

NORTH CHOIR AISLE

The North Choir Aisle and the southern are both walled off from the choir itself. One of the screens that used to divide the monastic from the parochial part of

[12] Sam. xiv. 4-14; xviii. 1-4; xxxi. 2.
[13] 1 Macc. iii. 12; ix. 10; ix. 18.

the church halves the four bays of the north aisle, the door in it being approached by a flight of eight wooden steps, which cover those of stone so worn by the passage of the pilgrims who in old times thronged to St. William's shrine. The westernmost door in the north wall formerly gave access to Gundulf's tower, the easternmost now leads to the belfry.

Monuments.—Coming from the north transept we see, to the right, the tomb ascribed to Bishop Hamo de Hythe, who died in 1352. It is certainly in the style of that time. The elaborate ornamentation of the arch under the canopy is worthy of attention. At the back, beneath the canopy, is the demi-figure of an angel, holding a shield, but the high, panelled tomb has lost its effigy, if it ever bore one. The monument has suffered much, but still bears many traces of colour. Just opposite it is a mural monument commemorative of William Streaton, who died in 1609, after having been no less than nine times mayor of the city.

In the plain stone pavement there are crowded together, to the west of the steps, as many as eleven matrices of brasses.

ORGAN

The Organ, on the screen beneath the choir arch, owes its present form to Sir G. Scott, who divided it, placing half at either end of the screen, and thus preserved the vista of the choir, when he designed the new case.

In early times we read of the gift of an organ by Bishop Gilbert de Glanvill and that, during the terrible visitation of Simon de Montfort's troops, the "organs were raised in the voice of weeping." Such casual references are all that we find before the seventeenth century. In 1634, however, Archbishop Laud is informed of a recent great expenditure on the "making of the organs." This new purchase narrowly escaped rough usage at the hands of the Roundhead soldiery in 1642, for the troops, in their journey into Kent, left "the organs to be pluckt downe" on their return, but found them, then, already removed, of course with more gentle handling than they themselves would have used. The instrument was soon set up again after the Restoration, and Pepys, on April 10th, 1661, heard "the organs then a-tuning." In 1688, £160 was spent on its renovation and on a new "chair organ," a smaller, portable form. In 1791 a fine new organ was constructed by Greene, which stood over the middle of the screen and its case, with pinnacles, etc., "in the Gothic style" was designed by the Rev. — Ollive. This instrument was added to by Hill towards the middle of the present century at Canon Griffith's expense. The choir arch, above, continued draped until Scott's time, though many complained of the tawdriness of this decoration, which hid also from the nave the vaulting of the choir.

TOMB OF BISHOP HAMO DE HYTHE

(From A Drawing By R. J. Beale).

CHOIR SCREEN

The Organ Screen, at the head of the flight of ten steps by which the higher level of the choir is reached, has had its face towards the nave decorated recently, in memory of the late Dean Scott, joint compiler of the famous lexicon. The four figures on each side of the original fourteenth century doorway, represent, in order from the left, St. Andrew, King Ethelbert, St. Justus, St. Paulinus, Bishop Gundulf, the sacrist William de Hoo, Bishop Walter de Merton, and Cardinal John Fisher. The whole was designed by Mr. John Pearson, R.A., and the statues were executed, in Weldon stone, by Mr. Hitch. The work is careful, but it is amusing to notice that in the model held by Gundulf, and presumably intended for his own church, there appears the great Perpendicular window, now so prominent in the west front.

Sir Gilbert Scott had, with archæological correctness, left this side of the screen bare. It was kept so originally on account of the position before it of the other screen, the one against which St. Nicholas' altar stood. Earlier attempts than the present one have, however, been made to ornament it. In 1730 an order was given for the face towards the nave to be wainscoted, and in the "Gentleman's Magazine" for October, 1798, we read a criticism of some work then just carried out. We are told of pointed arches and tracery merely punched out, of crockets and finials barely hinted without any fine forms or beautiful relief, and of the lack of any "deep-shadowed infinity of mouldings."

CHOIR AND CHOIR TRANSEPT

The Choir is entered through the iron gates in the central doorway of the screen. The height of its floor above that of the nave is due to the splendid crypt on which it stands. It is all, excepting one or two features which we must point out later, in the Early English style, and was finished early in the thirteenth century.

Very noticeable to everyone coming into this part of the church is the great, some think excessive, use made of the famous dark marble from the quarries of Purbeck, in the vaulting and other shafts, in their bands, and in the string-courses that divide the stories. These, though now so dull, will admit of a high polish, but, unfortunately, do not retain it long. A small specimen in the south choir transept shows how beautiful the polished stone is. Polishing would probably also relieve them of their present rather heavy effect. The shafts generally spring from the ground, from bases of the coarser Petworth or Bethersden marble, and some of them have caps of hard stone. Above the choir stalls the main groups of vaulting shafts rise from finely carved brackets, of which two are here illustrated (pp. 88, 91), and the intermediate single ones from carved corbel heads, all of the same fine material as the shafts themselves. Some of these ornaments were, when uncovered in 1840, "very skilfully restored in mastic by Mr. Hamerton, a sculptor in the employ of Mr. Cottingham."

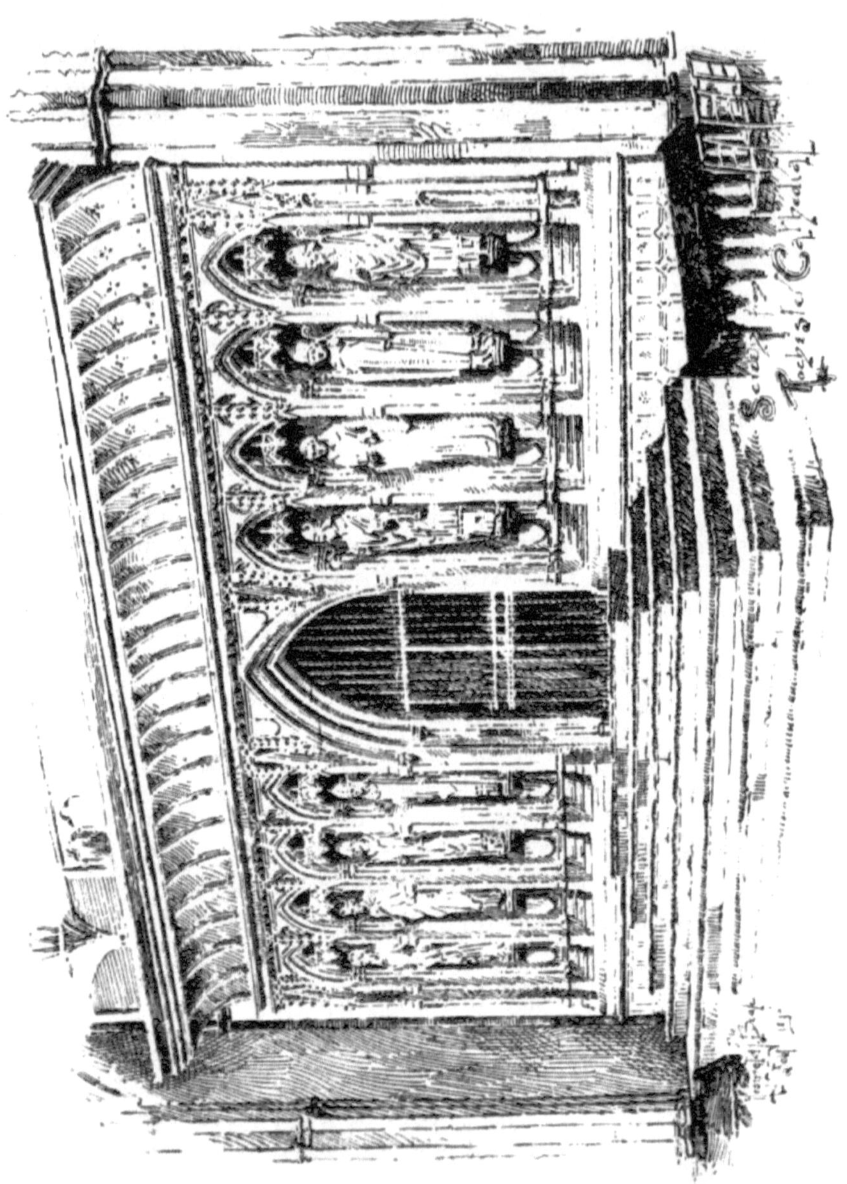

THE CHOIR SCREEN: DEAN SCOTT MEMORIAL

(From A Drawing By R. J. Beale).

The vaulting is worthy of attention and is generally sexpartite in plan, although the simpler quadripartite form occurs in places. An inequality in the division of the side cells of the transept vaulting, due to the difference in width of the bays, has a rather curious effect. The ribs of the vaulting, throughout the eastern arm, are painted with simple lines of colour, with a rather pleasing effect.

THE CHOIR, LOOKING EAST

(From A Photograph By Messrs. Carl Norman And Co.).

The gallery before the single light clerestory windows gave once an open passage all round, but it is now blocked at the end of the south transept. In front of each window it has a triple screen of which the general form is shown in our illustration of a window of the choir proper and in our view of the east end. It is owing to the existence over the transept aisles of two rooms, known as the Treasury and the Indulgence Chamber, that no clerestory windows are to be seen there, but only blind arcading and blank wall. In the inner, wider bays of the transepts we notice that the usual triple screens are extended by two additional arches of the lower height towards the centre of the church.

The clerestory gallery is, on each side of the choir proper, quite in the thickness of the wall. The core of the latter is Norman, but its facing, including the blind arcade at the triforium level, belongs to the Early English period.

On either side of the presbytery the clerestory gallery springs from wall-piers with clustered Purbeck shafts. The tracery of the windows, thus ornamented here, is later than the windows themselves, and is an insertion of the Decorated period. So is also that of the windows on the east side, and at the end, of the south transept aisle. The latter is unique in this cathedral, and we have thought it worthy of illustration. Remains of clustered columns, to be seen in the east wall of the north transept aisle, remind us of the numerous changes that so many parts of the fabric have undergone.

The east end has only taken its present form since Sir G. Scott's work, between 1870 and 1875. In 1825 Cottingham removed a huge altar screen thence, and opened and renewed the lower range of windows, of which the central had been quite, and the other two partly, blocked with brickwork. He, however, still left the communion table against the wall, and, instead of doing away with the great upper window then existing, only repaired it. This great window, occupying the whole space from the gallery to the vaulting, was divided into nine lights, of which the inner seven were cut by a transom or horizontal mullion. Photographs of three drawings by Mr. Gunning, made in 1842, are preserved in the chapter room, and show this east end, and the two sides of the organ screen, as they were before Scott's alterations.

Pavement

The north transept end is very like the east end in its general design, but has, low down, the two windows lighting the Merton tomb, and the tiny one over the same bishop's Elizabethan effigy. The south transept end is again much the same, but has the spaces between the wall-piers and under its outer windows filled in with masonry, in which are the openings to two passages, now blocked, which led respectively up to the Indulgence Chamber and down to the crypt.

There are three other doorways, the uses of which we must also mention. One at the north-west corner of the north transept leads to the staircase in the angle turret there; another, on the other side of the transept, is the way to the Treasury, to the clerestory gallery, and, by the gallery, to the Indulgence Chamber. The third is the splendid chapter-house doorway in the south transept aisle. To this one a special section will presently be devoted.

We have spoken more than once of the Treasury and the Indulgence Chamber. The latter is little used now, if at all, possibly because of the rather adventurous approach to it; but in the former the cathedral plate is still kept.

CORBEL IN CHOIR (H. P. CLIFFORD DEL.).

In the **Paving** of the choir there is a considerable variety. Up the choir proper we see slabs of variously coloured stones arranged in a not very elaborate pattern, part of the north transept and the whole of its aisle are also paved with stones of different colours "beautifully disposed," and there is a similar but simpler flooring behind the altar. To nearly all the rest of the eastern arm was given by Sir G. Scott a glittering floor of encaustic tiles; but much of the pavement of the south transept and its aisle is still of plain stone. The tiles have mostly old designs, taken from some mediæval examples still to be seen in the south choir transept and under an arch on the east side of the northern. To the east of the crossing is the matrix of a fine brass, of a bishop in full robes with mitre and crosier, with two shields of arms on each side of the figure. Farther on, between the altar and its rails, the tiling is very elaborate and, in a ring of it there, the signs of the zodiac appear. At the top of the dark marble altar steps there are tiles again. Those in front have representations of the seven virtues, and two others, with angels, are to be seen on each side.

A WINDOW, CHOIR CLERESTORY

(From A Drawing By H. P. Clifford).

Stalls

The Stalls of the dean and canons stand against the organ screen and face towards the east. They were designed, in the Gothic style, by Sir G. Scott, and have no canopies on account of the painted decoration above. The choir stalls also owe their present form to Scott, but he incorporated in them as much old work as possible. The seats against the wall on each side (the misericords) are all new, but not so are the trefoil-headed arcade and the massive oak beam which bear the standards supporting their book-rests. This arcade still has some of its original colouring, and belongs probably to the original furniture of the choir at the time of its completion, early in the thirteenth century. Many sections of the heavy beam above are also old, perhaps of the same age. The backs of the front row of seats, bearing the book-rests to the middle row, are chiefly constructed of old Tudor panelling, which once belonged to the book-desks made for the new establishment in 1541. Tracing the history of the furniture from this time, we find Archbishop Laud, in 1634, ordering a new fair desk to be provided without delay. After the Civil War considerable repairs were no doubt needed, but it is not until 1742-43 that we find any great works undertaken. Wainscoting and pews were then erected, and we read of a furnishing of choir seats, and of stalls for the dean and prebendaries under the organ. Only slight alterations were made in these by Mr. Cottingham, but they were, in 1840, cleared of paint under his direction, and "beautifully grained as panel oak." Finally, in 1870-75, they were done away with by Scott, whose new stalls were, together with other interior fittings of the choir, paid for with a sum of £3,000 generously given by Dr. and Mrs. Griffith, to whom the cathedral was already greatly indebted.

The old pews mentioned above rose in tiers, high and plain, on either side of the central alley, and the wainscoting behind them shut off the transepts, turning them into separate chapels. They and it were only removed in 1867.

Paintings

Decorative Mural Painting.—On removing the panelling at the back of the old choir stalls, Sir Gilbert Scott found that the whole length of the walls had once been painted. The old stalls were fortunately so high that they had saved not only the lower border, which, with its ribbon pattern and yellow six-petalled roses, is the same on each wall, but nearly a complete row of the main design as well. Scott retained this, and repeated it over the rest of the space, up to the top border, of which traces remained just under the first string-course. This upper border varies slightly on the different sides. The shields in it, formerly blank, are now occupied with the coats-of-arms of bishops of the see.

The pattern that covers the space between the borders is certainly heraldic. The lions in the red quatrefoils, and the fleurs-de-lis in the alternate blue spaces, correspond in every possible way—in form, colour, and ground—with those of the royal arms of England and of France. Dating, as they almost certainly do, from the fourteenth century, they remind us of the attempts of Edward III. and his brave son to unite both realms under his sway. The idea of the design may have come from Canterbury, where an earlier border, of similar materials, alluded perhaps to Edward II.'s marriage with Isabella of France. After making this suggestion, Canon Scott Robertson[14] records a mention of the use, at much the same time, of a similarly constituted pattern on some altar-cloths at Westminster Abbey.

WINDOW TRACERY, S. CHOIR TRANSEPT AISLE
(H. P. Clifford Del.).

The painting is continued on oak panelling across the organ screen. A piece of

---

[14] "Archæologia Cantiana," x. 70.

the original panelling, with a fragment of an earlier rather tartan-like pattern also, is now hung, under glass, on a pier opposite the chapter-house door.

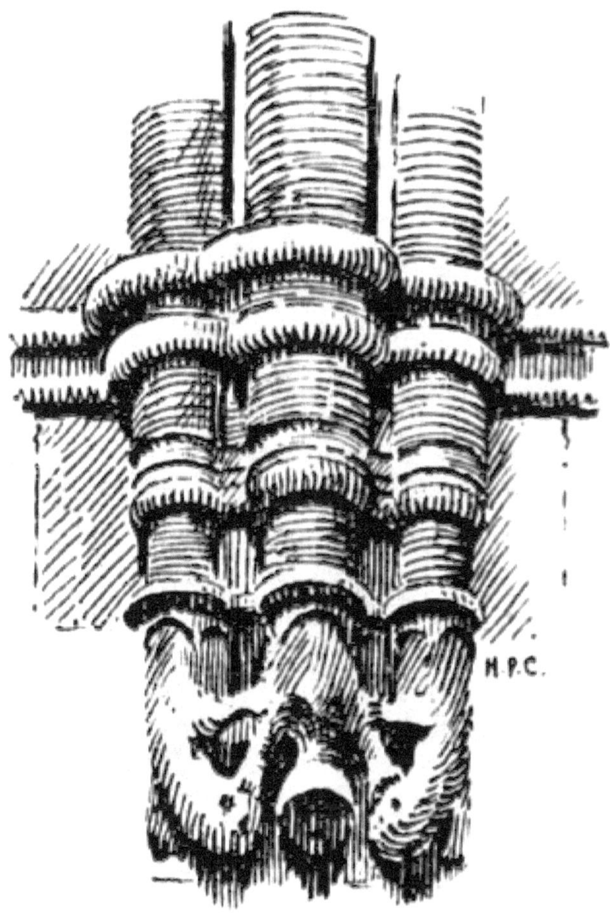

CORBEL IN CHOIR

(H. P. Clifford Del.).

Bishop's Throne

The Bishop's Throne, on the south side, just to the west of the crossing, is of carved oak, in the Gothic style, and has a rich canopy. It was designed by Scott, and was a present to the cathedral from Lord Dudley, a brother-in-law of Bishop Claughton. Of two of its predecessors some particulars can be given. In 1743 Bishop Wilcocks gave a throne, classical in style, with a flat pedimental canopy supported by massive columns. The place of this was taken in 1840 by a new work of Cottingham's, which was still more quickly supplanted by the present throne. Cottingham's did not, however, long remain unused; it was taken to St. Albans in 1877 for the enthronement of Dr. Claughton as the first bishop of that new see.

THE BISHOP'S THRONE

(From A Drawing By R. J. Beale).

On the north wall, directly opposite the bishop's throne, there still remains a portion, about 5 ft. 10 in. high and 2 ft. 2 in. wide, of an old fresco painting of that favourite mediæval subject, **The Wheel of Fortune**. This was uncovered when the older pulpit was taken down to make room for Mr. Cottingham's in 1840. At that time, we are told, the background had a diaper of small flowers, and there was the outline of a shield above, in which, however, no charges could be traced. Fortune, pictured as a queen, is robed in yellow, and regulates the movement of her wheel, of the same colour, with her right hand. It is interesting to trace the changes in the dress of the other figures. At her feet a man, plainly clad in a dark red gown, with green stockings and black shoes, is trying to gain a position on the wheel. Above this poor struggling one we see one who has risen halfway to the summit, and whose attire is correspondingly richer. His gown is a little lighter in colour, and has a hood to match; his sleeves are yellow, his stockings green, and his shoes ornamented. At the top is proudly and comfortably seated the present favourite, richly arrayed in a full robe of red turned up with white, with furs round his neck, a white belt and green hose. He looks towards the missing half of the picture, where others were no doubt represented as falling or fallen from the high place that he now holds, and his countenance seems to express mingled satisfaction and inquietude.

This fresco dates probably from as far back as the thirteenth century. Attempts have been made to attach a more particular interpretation to it, to make it represent the rapid rise of Gundulf, for instance; but it seems correct to give it a general signification, to look on it as typical of the uncertainty and changeableness of earthly things.

Pulpit and Lectern

The Pulpit, of plain wood, designed by Sir G. Scott, stands at the north-east corner of the crossing. Its predecessor, by Cottingham, used to be directly in front of the bishop's throne, and is now in the nave. **The Lectern**, of brass, and in the well-known eagle form, is a gift from Bishop Claughton, and the stand to it was presented by Dean Scott.

Altar and Sedilia

The Altar stands, it will be noticed, some distance in front of the east end, and there is a free passage all round. This position was proved to be archæologically correct when Sir G. Scott lowered the floor of this part of the church. The reredos, one of the fittings provided by Dr. and Mrs. Griffith, and designed by Scott, projects beyond the altar-table on each side in a way that is unusual and not altogether pleasing. It is of Caen stone, and contains a representation of the Last Supper in rather high relief, within a three-gabled canopy. The dark marble columns supporting the central gable are beautifully veined.

THE WHEEL OF FORTUNE

(From A Drawing By H. P. Clifford).

The altar seems to have kept its old position until 1634, when Laud, greatly shocked, gave orders to "place the communion-table at the end of the choir in a decent manner, and make a fair rail to go across the aisle as in other cathedral church-es." The dean and chapter protested slightly, pointing out that, if placed quite at the end it would be almost out of hearing of the congregation, and suggested as an alternative the erection of a screen behind it where it then stood. In 1642 some soldiers of the Parliament visited the cathedral, moved the altar, broke up the steps on which it was raised, and tore down its rails, leaving the wood as firing for the poor. Repairs must have been needed here, therefore, when the Restoration came. Later, by a chapter act of the 2nd June, 1707, the clerk was empowered to sign an agreement with a Mr. Coppinger for a new altar-piece, which seems to have been still in existence in 1788, and to be the one then described as of Norway oak, plain and neat, by the Rev. S. Denne. A resolution had been passed a little before, on the 6th December, 1706, that "the piece of rich silk and silver brocade given by the Bishop of Rochester should be put up." If applied to the new altar-piece this did not last long, for in 1752 a large piece of rich velvet, in a frame elegantly carved and gilt, was purchased with £50 given by Archbishop Herring, a former dean, to take the place of the central panel of plain wainscot. This was itself removed in 1788, when a picture by Sir Benjamin West, P.R.A., "The Angels appearing to the Shepherds," was inserted in its stead. This picture was presented anonymously, but the name of the donor, J. Wilcocks, Esq., a son of the bishop, transpired after his death. When Mr. Cottingham removed the old "Corinthian" altar-piece, West's work was, in 1826, lent to St. Mary's church, Chatham, on the condition that it should be returned when no longer needed. Archdeacon Laws was then rector. A later rector, Canon Jelf, was, in 1886, able to announce to his vestry that the dean and chapter waived all their rights, so the picture is still to be seen hanging over the vestry door. It cannot be called a great work, and we can scarcely wonder that it was thought by many unworthy of its high place in the cathedral.

The three great panels of **Mosaic** occupying the lower part of the east end, behind the altar, are a memorial to Mrs. Scott, the wife of the late dean. When the whitewash was scraped off, after the removal of the altar-piece in 1825, this wall was found to have been enriched with elaborate decorative paintings "of birds and beasts, fleurs-de-lis, lilies, crescents, stars, scroll foliage, fleury crosses, lace work borders, etc., arranged in most beautiful order and finely contrasted in colours, which consist of the brightest crimsons, purples, azures, greens, etc."

The fine **Piscina** in the easternmost bay on the north side, just behind the altar, deserves notice. Its recess has a richly cusped arch, and in the wall below is a curi-ous cupboard, intended probably for the sacramental vessels.

The Sedilia stand on the other side, in the third bay from the east. The stalls are of stone, three in number, and in date late Perpendicular. The arms on their canopies are those of the see of Rochester, of the Priory of St. Andrew, Rochester, and of that of Christ Church, Canterbury. Within the sedilia, at one time often mis-named "confessionals," painted figures of bishops were formerly visible, even within the present century. The brass book-rest at the foot of the polished mar-ble steps in front was given in Dean Scott's memory by his sons and daughters. Opposite, on the other side of the chancel, stands a richly carved episcopal chair upholstered with blue velvet.

Communion Plate

The Communion Plate is still kept in an old iron-bound chest in the "Treasury," over the north choir transept aisle.

The chief service, consisting of two cups with covers, two flagons, an alms-dish and two patens with covers, was made for James, Duke of Lenox and Richmond, in London in 1653-54. Sir Joseph Williamson, a later resident at Cobham Hall bequeathed it to the cathedral by his will of 1701. The whole service was gilt, and the bequest included also a pair of magnificent pricket candlesticks, each nearly 20 inches high, with rich stems and massive scrolled bases. It is described by Canon Scott Robertson in "Archæologia Cantiana," vol. xvi., and illustrated in vol. xvii.

Two other gilt cups and two patens, made at London in 1662-63, were given to the cathedral by Dr. R. Cooke, who had, the inscriptions tell us, become a prebendary in 1660. Each cup has engraved on it a copy of the common seal of the dean and chapter, with Dr. Cooke's arms above. The button bases of the patens bear the donor's crest.

The oldest and most interesting pieces at Rochester are, however, two alms-basins or patens (perhaps originally ciboria), made at London in 1530-31. The insides of the bowls, except the nearly vertical rims, are embossed with a honeycomb pattern, and beneath each hexagon here, there is a plain circle outside. The knops are ornamented with flowers and half-flowers, and the stems beneath have each a frilled collar and a pattern in repoussé of overlapping scales or leaves. The foot, under a cable moulding, is beaten into an egg-and-tongue pattern. One has on its rim, in Lombardic capitals, the inscription, *Benedicamus Patrem et Filium cum Sancto Spiritu*, and the other, the same except for the curious contraction, *Sper.*, for the last word. There is also a cover of silver gilt, which was made at London in 1532-33. Its button handle has four supports, moulded like cords, and it is itself decorated in repoussé.

One solitary survivor of the old monastic plate remains, and some mention of it seems appropriate here. We allude to the famous **Rochester mazer**, made in 1532, and given to the refectory *per fratrem Robertum Pecham*. This is now in the possession of Sir A. W. Franks, by whom it was acquired at the sale of the Fontaine collection at Narford Hall. It is illustrated in "Archæologia," xxiii., 393, and described by Mr. St. John Hope in the same publication, vol. 1., 168.

Monuments

Monuments, etc.—When the great bishop, Walter de Merton, died, in 1772, a sumptuous monument was erected over his remains at the end of the north choir transept. His executors' accounts give us particulars as to the cost. The chief feature was the enamel work by Jean de Limoges, who was paid £40 5*s.* 6*d.* for executing it, bringing it over and setting it up. The balance between this sum and the total amount of £67 14*s.* 6*d.* was paid for the rich, vaulted canopy and other masonry, the two stained glass windows and the iron railing.

This tomb suffered much at the time of the Reformation, and the Merton College authorities undertook its repair, during Sir Henry Savile's wardenship, in 1598. It was then opened, and the body of the bishop, who had been buried in his robes, with his pastoral staff and chalice, disclosed. The staff on being touched fell to pieces but the chalice was removed to the college to be treasured there. The original enamelled work seems to have been injured beyond repair, so was replaced by the alabaster effigy now in the next bay. This effigy is remarkable for the anachronisms it shows. The bishop wears the rochet, the episcopal dress of the Reformed church instead of his proper robes, and the plain crook beside him bears no resemblance to the rich crosiers of the thirteenth century. The ruff round his neck and his broad-toed shoes are also plainly out-of-date. The mantle of estate refers of course to his rank as Chancellor, as did also the bag or purse that used to hang on the wall above. The inscriptions were on the front of the tomb, whence came also the death's head panels to be seen with the effigy now.

Fresh injuries, suffered during the Civil War period, were made good by the college in 1662, and a tablet recording this, and balanced by the bishop's arms, was placed at the back of the tomb where the windows had been blocked up. There were fresh renovations in 1701, and in 1770, when all the whitewash was cleaned off. The College also made an annual payment for care of the tomb.

The monument received its present form in 1849, when the Elizabethan effigy and details, and the old railing, were removed to the next bay, where they are still to be seen. The skeleton was then once more uncovered showing the bishop to have been a fine tall man, and a trace of the former opening of the tomb was found in a misplacement of the bones of the right arm, which had probably been disturbed when the chalice was removed. Fragments of wood and cloth, presumably remains of his staff and robes, were still to be seen. The two windows under the canopy were reopened and filled with stained glass, and on the tomb was placed a stone slab, "engraved according to the style of the thirteenth century," with an ornamented cross having foliations on each side. "A new ornamental railing," coloured and gilt, and of a tawdry character was placed in front of all. The canopy, with its crockets and pinnacles, and the quatrefoils of carved foliage in its gables are worthy of attention.

The tomb in the easternmost bay of the transept end is reputed to be that of St. William of Perth, the great Rochester saint. This transept formed his chapel, and his shrine is believed to have stood on a slab marked with six crosses, that lay in the centre of the floor until the present elaborate pavement was put down. Lambarde gives the following account of the saint, saying that he derives it from the "Nova Legenda" itself. "He was by birth, a Scot, of Perthe (now commonly called Saint Johns Town), by trade of life a Baker of bread and thereby got his living: in charity so aboundant, that he gave to the poore the tenth loafe of his workmanship: in zeale so fervent, that in vow he promised, and in deede attempted, to visit the holy land (as they called it) and the places where Christ was conversant on earth: in which journey, as he passed through Kent, hee made Rochester his way: where after that he had rested two or three daies he departed toward Canterbury. But ere he had gone farre from the Citie, his servant that waited on him, led him (of purpose) out of the high way, and spoiled him both of his money and life. This done, the servant escaped, and the Maister (bicause he died in so holy a purpose of minde) was by the Monkes conveied to Saint Andrewes, (and) laide in the quire." In Baring-Gould's "Lives of the Saints" (under May 23rd) we read that the murderer was a foundling, who had been brought up out of charity by him whom he slew. The pilgrim's death occurred in 1201, and soon "he moalded miracles plentifully" at his tomb, so plentifully that with the offerings consequently there made, the choir of the cathedral was completed, ready for the solemn entry in 1227. His fame continued to grow so much, that in 1266 Bishop Lawrence de St. Martin went to Rome and procured his canonization, and he did not pass out of repute until Protestant times. The high coffin tomb, of dark marble, has on its lid a foliated cross in relief, and on its front four circular medallions with crosses of four sculptured leaves. The arch of the recess, springing from corbels of elaborately carved foliage, retains traces of colouring, and the wall within is painted with green foliated scroll-work on a dark red ground.

Under the northern arch on the east side of the transept is the curious sarcophagus tomb of Bishop Lowe, who died in 1467. This stood, until the time when the transept was thrown open, against the centre of the wainscot that separated the chapel of St. William from the choir. The arms on the shield at the end of the front are those of the bishop, and they occur again, borne by an angel carved in relief, on the right end, impaling there the coat of the see on the sinister side.

We pass now to the railed-off transept aisle, known as St. John the Baptist's Chapel, or as the Warner Chapel from the three seventeenth century monuments that it contains. These are all in the "Palladian" style in vogue at that time, and constructed chiefly of touch (black marble) and white marble. They are in memory of Bishop John Warner (d. 1666), of his nephew Archdeacon John Lee Warner (d. 1679), and of the latter's eldest son, Lee Warner, Esq. (d. 1698). The bishop's monument is signed by the sculptor, Jos. Marshall, of London.

In the same chapel, in a recess beside Bishop Warner's monument, is an old and weather-worn statue traditionally said to represent the great architect-bishop Gundulf. This was brought hither by Mr. Pearson, when he rebuilt the north-west tower, in the lower arcade of which it had been carefully replaced in the changes of about 1770. The mitre is almost lost, the face has suffered greatly, and the hands, feet and parts of the crosier are quite gone. The chasuble hangs in curious, close, U-like folds and the crosier staff passes diagonally across the body. From an etching published in the "Journal of the British Archæological Association," in 1853, when the sculpture was, of course, less worn than now, there seems to be under the chasuble a dalmatic, and then under the dalmatic an alb over which the ends of the stole appear.

Under the arch between the aisle and the choir, is the most remarkable of all the monuments in the church, the tomb of Bishop John de Sheppey. Its very existence had long been forgotten, when Mr. Cottingham, in 1825, removed the chalk and masonry, with which it had for many years been covered and concealed. Whether this covering was to save it from the Roundhead soldiery or from earlier iconoclastic reformers is not known. Alluding to the bishop, Bishop Weever wrote, in 1631, "his portraiture is in the wall over his place of buriall." We have here an evident reference to this effigy, and I think that Weever probably used "in" in its most literal sense, implying that "the portraiture" was already walled up in this time, though it has been taken to express merely the position within an arch of the choir wall. If the effigy had been long hidden the mere tradition of its existence might have died out during the troubled period between 1640 and 1660, but if it had been open to view in the earlier of these years it is not likely that all recollection of it would have passed so quickly away. We must remember too that this monument is more perfect than most others in the cathedral; and that they suffered, as we have already told, the greatest damage in early Protestant times. It seems, therefore, only reasonable to suppose that this most gorgeous of all had been already hidden and protected. So universal was destruction then and earlier, that in the second year of her reign Queen Elizabeth found it necessary to issue a stringent proclamation "against breakinge or defacing of monuments of Antiquitie, being set up in Churches or other publique places for memory and not for superstition."

The bishop's effigy lies, where it was found, on a high tomb with panelled sides, each having seven recesses separated by tiny buttresses. The canopy, ogee-shaped above, and with a plain elliptical arch below, was much mutilated, but seems to have been crocketed and terminated by a finial. It owes its present form to Mr. Cottingham, who restored it in 1840.

The effigy itself has been much praised, and deservedly. The sculpture, in stone, is excellent, and the colours have a fine effect. It is surprising to see how general is the belief that this is "probably the most perfect specimen of ancient colouring now existing in England," and how even great authorities refer to "its very perfect original colouring;" for in the "Gentleman's Magazine" (September, 1825) we can read how the monument was treated just after its discovery. A Mr. Harris, in Mr. Cottingham's employ, made two drawings of the effigy, one showing it as it was, the other as the architect thought it had been. The restoration of the colours, according to the second drawing, was then resolved on and carried out, and, as a result, "the dalmatic, instead of being a pink, is now a dull scarlet, with a *green lining*, and the shoes are painted *yellow*." Matters are still worse when we see Mr. Harris complaining (in a letter now at the British Museum) that the renovation according to his drawing was done "by an unskilful hand, consequently the remains of the beautiful colouring were destroyed, which was much regretted by the dean, Dr. Stevens, at the time." The sculpture seems fortunately not to have been tampered with; some fragments luckily discovered were fitted in their places, but no further restoration was attempted. These fragments were the top of the mitre, most of the fingers, the feet, and the head of one of the little dogs lying thereby.

The bishop's face, naturally coloured like the rest of the effigy, is rather mutilated, but seems to have been close shaven. Under his outermost robe, the chasuble, comes the dalmatic, through the side openings of which the rich green of the tunic appears. The colour of the latter robe used, however, to be scarcely visible. The ends of the stole do not appear, but, under all, the alb hangs down to the feet. The apparel of the alb, the amice round his neck, and the maniple of his left arm are shown as richly embroidered with gold. The bishop wears jewelled gloves, and on the fourth finger of his left hand the episcopal ring, of gold set with a ruby. His head, with the precious mitre, rests on two cushions, and finally against his left shoulder lies the splendid crosier, of which, unfortunately, the crook is gone.

TOMB OF BISHOP JOHN DE SHEPPEY

(From A Photograph By J. L. Allen).

On the side towards the choir, of the slab on which he rests, we read "HIC IACET DNS IOHANS DE SCHEPEIE EPUS HUIUS ECCLIE." The same words appear on the other side, except that ISTIUS takes the place of HUIUS, a change which implies some independence in the chapel.

The railing before the tomb perhaps belonged to it originally. Along the upper band should be noticed the curious pounced pattern, and its three massive lily spikes cannot but attract attention. It was the occurrence of the letters I s, the bishop's initials, just under the central spike, that led to the railing being brought hither from another part of the church.

A rare set of six lithographs, published by Mr. Cottingham, to which the text seems never to have been printed, shows us the monument as it was when found. Its present appearance can be judged, without a visit to Rochester, from the cast at the Crystal Palace, a fine set of drawings by Mr. Lambert at the South Kensington Museum, or the engravings published in an article by Mr. Kempe in the "Archæologia," vol. xxv. The author of this paper, which was read to the Society of Antiquaries only seven years after the restoration, seems to have been unaware of any thing of this sort having been attempted.

In the rubbish over the effigy some remarkable fragments of polychrome sculpture were found. These are still preserved in the crypt.

Passing along the north side of the church, we see in the third bay from the east end, the curious shrine-like monument of dark marble, ascribed to Bishop Gilbert de Glanvill, who died in 1214. A very similar monument at Canterbury was once the subject of much discussion, but has lately been opened and proved to be the tomb of the renowned Archbishop Hubert Walter. He and Gilbert were contemporaries and friends, so the ascription of the Rochester example to the latter is very probably correct.

In the next bay is a coffin-shaped tomb of dark marble, with the recumbent effigy of a bishop, whose features are much mutilated, and whose hands and feet are gone. This tomb is assigned, it seems rightly, to Bishop Lawrence de St. Martin (d. 1274). The canopy over the head of the effigy is a fine and rich example of architectural work of the Early Decorated style.

Behind the altar is a great slab, which once bore the effigies, in brass, of a lady and of a knight in armour. When the slab had to be removed, during the erection of the new reredos, a leaden coffin was found, and a female body closely wrapped in lead. The knight here buried was Sir William Arundel, K.G., governor of the city and castle of Rochester, whose will, dated 1st August, 1400, gave directions for his "body to be buried in the Priory at Rochester, at the back of the high altar." His lady, afterwards, in her will of the 6th September, 1401, arranged for her dead body to be laid "in the Priory of St. Andrews in Rochester, under the tomb where my husband and me are pictured." Sir Richard Arundel, a brother of Sir William, and the next constable of the castle, was possibly also buried in this church when he died in 1412. In his will of the 8th July, 1417, he had expressed the wish that his grave should be made in the Lady Chapel.

On the south side of the chancel, in the easternmost bay, is a plain, dark-coloured marble coffin, without any inscription or ornament. This is ascribed to Bishop Gundulf, who died in 1107, but as it is rectangular and not of the old coffin form, Mr. Bloxam thinks that it cannot be placed earlier than the fifteenth century. Gundulf's remains may, however, have been moved when the great eastward extension was made, and have been subsequently placed here. This would justify the tradition that the monument has contained his bones.

TOMBS OF BISHOPS GLANVILL AND ST. MARTIN

(From A Photograph By J. L. Allen).

In the next bay to the west we have a dark marble monument, very like that of Bishop Lawrence de St. Martin, and possibly even by the same artist. Its canopy is, however, simpler. This tomb seems to be correctly attributed to Bishop Inglethorp, who died in 1291.

Passing the sedilia we come to a peculiar, probably thirteenth century, coffin, which still contained a skeleton when it was found in the crypt under the north choir transept during the clearance of some rubbish in 1833. The lid rises in *dos d'âne* form, and along the ridge run two leafed rods, in relief, which bend outwards in scrolls, at the centre, just before they meet (see p. 105).

We now turn, finally, to notice another interesting stone coffin in the middle of the south choir transept end. This, also probably of the thirteenth century, has on its lid a cross in relief, the stem of which, with three pairs of curious drooping leaves, rises from a graduated base. This is probably one of two coffins, to which the Rev. S. Denne alludes as having existed in this part of the church. This, or the other, had been, he says, broken open by the Parliamentarians, and a chalice and crucifix removed therefrom.

Stained Glass

Stained Glass in the Choir.—The six windows of the east end were given, in 1873, by ladies and gentlemen of the neighbourhood. They celebrate the successive dedications of the church to St. Andrew, and to Christ and the Blessed Virgin Mary. The middle window of the upper range contains a representation of Our Lord in Glory, that of the lower tier the scene of his Ascension. On the right hand is a figure of the Blessed Virgin above a picture of the Nativity, while on the other side a figure of St. Andrew, and the Call of that Apostle and St. Peter, are to be seen.

CARVED COFFIN LID.

The four upper windows on the south side of the presbytery contain single figures of the four Evangelists, and commemorate, in order, Dean Stevens, T. H. Day, Esq., Mrs. Day and Mrs. Thorold. In the corresponding windows on the other side are pictured four writers of Epistles, St. Paul, St. James, St. Jude, and St. Peter.

It has been arranged that the four lower, three-lighted windows on the south side shall contain the twelve Apostles, one figure in each light. In the second from the east end we see (in memory of Alfred Smith, Esq.) St. John, St. Bartholomew, and St. Philip; and in the fourth (which commemorates Miss Nicholson), St. Jude, St. Simon, and St. Matthias appear. The others are still unfilled. The similar windows opposite illustrate scriptural allusions to Christ as the Good Shepherd. They are in memory of Dr. T. Robinson, Mrs. Griffith, General Travers, R.M., and Dr., once Canon Griffith; and show the Shepherd tending his sheep (St. John, x. 14-16); the Shepherd smitten and the sheep scattered (Zech., xiii. 7, St. Matt., xxvi. 31); the Crucifixion, where the Shepherd gives his life for the sheep (St. John, x. ii); and lastly, the Son of Man dividing the good from the evil, as a Shepherd divides the sheep from the goats (St. Matt., xxv. 31-46).

In St. John the Baptist's Chapel there is a single stained window, with our Lord's Ascension, in memory of Lieut. F. N. Hassard, R.E. Passing to the north transept we find the outer upper windows filled only with plain glass, while the middle one has a figure of St. Gregory, inserted in memory of Captain W. Walton Robinson, R.E., who died at Aden in 1887. The windows of the lower range contain figures of St. Gundulf, St. Paulinus, and Walter de Merton, and commemorate respectively Canon S. Dewe (d. 1885), Dr. G. Murray, Bishop of Sodor and Man and afterwards of Rochester (d. 1860), and Mrs. Maxwell Hyslop (d. 1888). Each of these four windows of the transept end contains a small scene beneath the single figure. The tiny light over Walter de Merton's Elizabethan effigy was glazed, after the recovery of Mr. Thomas Aveling from a serious illness, by his family, and illustrates the miracle of the healing of the nobleman's son.

All the glass described above is the work of Messrs. Clayton and Bell. The two plainer windows to the Merton tomb are by J. Miller.

Of the two windows in the south choir transept aisle, the first, by Gibbs, and given by the officers of the Royal Engineers in memory of their comrade, General Ballard, represents the Raising of Lazarus. The other, with Our Lord's Resurrection was given by the Rev. T. T. Griffith, precentor, in memory of Thos. Griffith, Esq., and was executed by Hardman.

The windows of the south choir transept are also by Clayton and Bell. Those of the upper tier commemorate Major S. Anderson, C.M.G., Capt. W. J. Gill, R.E., and Capt. J. Dundas, V.C., and their respective subjects are: Moses during the fight against Amalek (Exod., xvii. 11, 12), Joshua and the Captain of the Lord's Host (Josh., v. 13-15), and David advancing to do battle with Goliath (I. Sam., xvii. 48-49). Those of the lower range, — in memory of Major R. Hume, C.B., Capt. R. Nichols Buckle, R.E., and Capt. C. W. Innes, represent the centurion's appeal to Christ for his servant's healing (St. Luke, vii. 9), the Crucifixion, with the centurion at the foot of the Cross (St. Mark, xv. 39), and the appearance of the angel to another centurion, Cornelius, with the legend: "What is it, Lord (Acts, x. 4)."

Chapter House Doorway

The famous **Chapter House Doorway**, one of the finest pieces of English Decorated in existence, dates from the middle of the fourteenth century, probably from the episcopate of Hamo de Hythe.

The full-length figures, one on each side of the door, symbolizing the Church and the Synagogue, were both headless when Mr. Cottingham restored the doorway, between 1825 and 1830. Much fault has been found with him for turning the first, which is thought to have been like the other a female figure, into a mitred, bearded bishop holding a cross in his right hand and the model of a church in his left. The blindfolded "Synagogue," by her broken staff, and the tables of the law held reversed in her right hand, typifies the overthrow of the Mosaic dispensation. Above are figures, two on each side, seated at book desks under canopies. These are supposed to be the four great Doctors of the Church: Saints Augustine, Gregory, Jerome, and Ambrose. Quite at the head of the arch, under a lofty pyramidal canopy, we see a tiny nude figure which represents probably a pure soul just released from Purgatory. If this is so, it would account for the flames from which the angels, on each side, bearing scrolls, seem to be rising. It has been suggested likewise that the distorted heads, which alternate with squares of foliage in the wider inside moulding of the doorway typify the sufferings of the soul in its passage. The outside moulding is also interesting, being a wide hollow in the bottom of which circular holes are cut at intervals. Through these can be seen the broad stem from which spring the leaves that ornament the intervening spaces. The arch head is ogee-shaped outside, with large external, and smaller, but not less rich, internal crockets. The square back to it, and the spaces beneath the corbels, on which the Church and Synagogue figures stand, are filled with noteworthy diapers. The first is divided diagonally into sunken squares, each containing a flower; and the others have lion masks in quatrefoils, with five petalled roses in the alternate spaces.

The present door dates from Cottingham's time. He had found the archway partially blocked, so that an ordinary square-headed door might be inserted, a most barbarous arrangement. In the passage within is a portrait of Bishop Sprat, and in the **Chapter Room** itself one of King James I. and a view in St. Patrick's Cathedral, Dublin.

Chapter House and Library

The **Cathedral Library**, also contained in the Chapter Room, is a small, rather general collection, which, though increased from time to time by the dean and chapter, had no regular provision made for its increase until "an excellent regulation was made (some years before 1772) ... that every new dean and prebendary should give a certain sum of money, or books to that value, in lieu of those entertainments that were formerly made on their admission." This arrangement dates from the deanship of Dean Prat, who is recorded to have given a large book-case, which had once belonged to H.R.H. the Duke of York.

In the library there are several valuable bibles, including a copy of the famous first polyglot, known as the Complutensian, which was printed in six volumes at Alcala in Spain between 1502 and 1517, but was not published until 1522, owing probably to the death of its great promoter, Cardinal Ximenes. The Greek New Testament seems to have been first printed herein, though the edition of Erasmus (1516) forestalled it in publication. Brian Walton's Polyglot, published, also in six volumes, at London in 1657, is likewise on the shelves. Of rare English bibles the cathedral possesses a copy of Miles Coverdale's first complete edition in English (of 1535), of the rare and valuable Great Bible (Cranmer's) printed under Cromwell's patronage and published in 1539, and one of the first edition of Parker's or the Bishop's Bible, which dates from 1565. There is no early Book of Common Prayer, but a Missal (Salisbury use) of 1534 has been noticed.

THE CHAPTER HOUSE DOORWAY

(From A Photograph By Messrs. Carl Norman And Co.).

To turn now to manuscripts, disregarding the other classes of printed books, the cathedral possesses a great treasure in the **Textus Roffensis**, which is said to be the work of Bishop Ernulf and dates from early in the twelfth century. It contains old English codes of law, beginning with Ethelbert's, much ecclesiastical and historical information, records of privileges of the cathedral, and some interesting forms of excommunication, oaths, etc. In 1633 the dean (Dr. Balcanqual) and chapter had to obtain a bill in chancery to enforce its restitution by a Dr. Leonard who had got it into his possession. During the Civil Wars it was in the charge of Sir Roger Twysden and was used by Dugdale for his great work. The book was at London in 1712 for Dr. Harriss, a prebendary of the cathedral, to use for his "History of Kent" (published in 1719). It was taken thither and back by water, and on the return journey fell into the Thames. It was, fortunately, recovered, not much damaged, but was re-bound afterwards. Lambarde, as well as later historians, used it. Parts were printed by Wharton in his "Anglia Sacra" (1691) and by Willems in his "Leges Anglo-Saxonicæ" (1721). Hearne edited most of it, from a transcript by Sir Edward Dering, in 1720.

The **Custumale Roffense** (per fratrem J. de Westerham), another famous manuscript, dates from about 1300, its author, then a monk, became prior later, in Bishop Hamo's time. In this book is much information about manors and the priory's income from them, and it contains many interesting particulars of ancient tenures and rents, some details about the Rome-scot, notes as to the duties of various servants, etc. A printed edition of it, by Thorpe, appeared in 1788.

Two other manuscripts, relics of the old monastic library, have been found on the shelves, but the rest are scattered. This library must have been a rich one, for in a list, of as early as 1202, discovered by Mr. Rye in the Royal MSS. at the British Museum, there are as many as 241 works enumerated, mostly theological. Leland probably carried off many of them, since, out of eighty-six manuscripts in the British Museum, indexed there as having once belonged to the Rochester Monastery, no less than eighty-three are in the old Royal Collection. They are on vellum, partly illuminated, and many contain terrible anathemas against any who should deface or steal them. Two others have been found among Archbishop Parker's MSS. at Corpus Christi College, Cambridge, and one in Archbishop Laud's bequest to the Bodleian. The famous **Gundulf Bible** has an interesting history. All traces of it are lost between the time of the Suppression and 1734, when it was sold from the possession of a clergyman, Herman Van de Wall, at Amsterdam. Later, in the 1788 edition of the Custumale, we read that it had been again sold, not many years before, at Louvain, for 2,000 florins. It came back to England afterwards and, at the sale of the Rev. Theodore Williams in April, 1827, passed into the famous collection of Sir Thomas Phillipps for £189.

SOUTH CHOIR AISLE

Leaving the library we pass to the **South Choir Aisle**. This is twice as wide as that on the north side, and has acquired its present form by a curious series of changes. It was originally of the same width, and the south tower stood in the angle between it and the south transept. After the great twelfth century fires, a wall was carried eastwards from the middle of the tower to form the north side of the cloisters, which were then being repaired. A little later, possibly at the time when the south choir transept was built, the original aisle wall was removed and the whole space between the choir proper and the new cloister included in the aisle. The tower was not yet removed, in fact its demolition did not occur until about one hundred years later, towards the end of the thirteenth century. The present wooden roof was then erected, instead of a fine vaulting springing from a central pillar, which seems to have been originally intended.

TOMB OF BISHOP BRADFIELD

(From A Drawing By R. J. Beale).

The flights of twelve and ten steps, which together take up the whole width of the aisle, lead respectively, up to the eastern part of the church and down to the crypt. The wooden enclosure over the crypt entrance is used as a vestry. Two doors open into the south choir transept, one from the vestry and one directly from the aisle itself.

THE CRYPT, LOOKING TO THE NORTH-EAST

(From A Photograph By Messrs. Carl Norman And Co.).

The massive buttress supporting the choir wall, at the head of the steps to the undercroft, is divided into stages by a flat niche or panel with side-shafts of Purbeck marble. This was found, in 1840, to contain a mural painting of the Crucifixion, with the Blessed Virgin and St. John at the foot of the cross. The principal face below had a gigantic representation of the Madonna and Child, more than 12 feet in height. At about the same time the elegant little doorway at the west end of the aisle was found. It could not be reopened, but its mouldings were uncovered. It is of the Early English period and has a dripstone ending in a bishop's and a female head.

In this aisle, on its north side, is the tomb thought to be that of Bishop John de Bradfield, who is stated by Edmund de Hadenham to have been buried on the south side of the church, "juxta ostium excubitorum," *i.e.,* by the watchers' door. It has a very battered figure of a bishop in low relief.

CRYPT

The **Crypt**, or undercroft, is approached by the flight of steps in the south choir aisle, but its original entrance seems to have been on the other side of the church. Just inside the doorway, with its peculiar flatly-pointed head under a pointed arch, there is, to the right, a small square cell which may have been used as a place of confinement.

The crypt is one of the finest in England, and the later, main portion of it is the last great work of the kind carried out in this country. The two western severies, consisting of the old Norman work, are now shut off to contain the organ bellows and their machinery, and the whole southernmost aisle has been partitioned off into a series of new vestries, erected with the proceeds of Dean Hole's recent lecturing tour in America. The whole width is divided into seven aisles, three under the choir proper and two under each transept. Each seems to have had an altar at its east end; several piscinas still remain. The main walls above are carried by heavy masses of masonry, which rather break the vistas, while other masses help the usual columns to bear the steps on which the altar stands.

In the early Norman work extending for two bays from the west we see circular shafts, with rough, convex, cushion capitals, and the lower corners chamfered. The plain rubble cross-vaults here have no ribs but the groins are pinched down to make them more prominent. The rest of the crypt is Early English, with circular and octagonal columns both occurring and having quadripartite vaulting. The clever way in which the architects overcame the difficulty caused by differences of span is worthy of attention. On the vaults, traces of painting, of floral diapers, etc., can still be seen, and in "The New British Traveller" (1819) we have a description of a subject medallion then to be seen beneath St. William's Chapel. "In a circle is a representation of a vessel sailing, with a large fish in the water in front, and on one side the upper part of a monk, with his hands uplifted as in prayer," apparently an illustration of the story of Jonah.

In the crypt are preserved many interesting fragments, including the pieces of polychrome sculpture found with Bishop John de Sheppey's monument. The most important is a statue of Moses, who bears his name on the tablet of stone that he holds.

CHAPTER IV.

THE DIOCESE AND BISHOPS.

According to a curious legend,[15] widely circulated in the Middle Ages, the men of Rochester did not accord a patient hearing to St. Augustine when he first came thither to preach the Gospel. They, instead, used him rudely, and in mockery threw at him and hung on his dress a lot of fish-tails. In anger the saint prayed to God to avenge him on his persecutors and "the Lord smote them *in posteriora* to their everlasting ignominy, so that not only on their own but on their successors' persons similar tails grew ever after." A way of escape was, however, according to the fourteenth century prose version of the "Brut," soon provided, for "whenne the kyng herde and wiste of this vengeance that was falle thurghe saynt Austines powere he lette make one howse in honour of God ... at the brugges end," children born in which would not be afflicted with the dreaded appendage. Other versions of the story give Dorchester as the place where the saint was thus ill-used and his assailants were thus punished, but both Kent and Dorset have been zealous to repudiate any concern with it, and Lambarde in his "Perambulation" has written an indignant diatribe in defence of the former county.

Later, in the legends concerning St. Thomas à Becket, another form of the same fable appears. The men of Strood are said to have docked the tail of his horse and to have been punished in the same way as St. Augustine's persecutors. In the story Rochester sometimes appears instead of Strood, and this is our excuse for alluding to the variation here. It seems to be due to a confusion of the old story with a new fact, as we have a contemporary statement that St. Thomas, on the Christmas Day before his death, excommunicated a certain Robert de Broc, because the latter had, to insult and shame him, cut off the tail of a mare in his service.

In the Middle Ages the matter was of national concern, for the disgrace said to have befallen the inhabitants of one or other of the small towns mentioned became "a scandal to their unoffending country." When the story spread, as it did, nearly all over Europe, foreigners did not particularize, but offensively alluded to all Englishmen as *caudati*, or tailed. Such allusions often occur in narratives of the Crusades, and the French and Scotch were especially keen to hurl the epithet at their hereditary foes. Even in the sixteenth century John Bale says, "that an Englyshman now can not travayle in an other land by waye of merchandyce or any other honest occupyenge, but yt ys most contumelyouslye throwne in his tethe that all Englishmen have tayles." The name "Kentish Longtails" seems to have been early current,

[15] This account of it is chiefly taken from a paper by G. Neilson, first published in "Transactions of the Glasgow Archæological Society," 1896.

and in Drayton's "Polyolbion" we find "Longtails and Liberty" given almost as a motto for the county.

We are not told whether it was due to this miracle of the "tails," but it is certain that the conversion of the townspeople of Rochester must have been rapid, for we know that a see was founded here as early as 604. The diocese placed under its bishop's care was a small one, including no more than the western part of the ancient kingdom of Kent, the dividing line being roughly the course of the Medway, or, more precisely, that of its tributary, the Teise. The whole diocese formed only a single archdeaconry, which was divided into four deaneries, and of this small number one was subject, as a peculiar, to the jurisdiction of the Archbishop of Canterbury, "who holdeth his prerogative wheresoever his lands do lye."

Not only "hath the See at Rochester well holden her owne: for during the whole succession of ... Bishops, which in right line have followed Justus, she hath continually mainteined her Chaire at this one place, whereas in most partes of the Realme besides, the Sees of the Bishops have suffred sundry translations," but it was long also before the ancient limits of the diocese were changed. In 1845 it was enlarged so as to include Essex and Hertfordshire, and was then divided into the four archdeaconries of Rochester, Colchester, Essex and St. Alban's. The old palace at Bromley, which had been since Cardinal Fisher's time the chief home of the bishops, was at the same time quitted for Danbury in Essex. In 1863 the archdeaconries of Rochester and St. Albans were joined into one, and in 1867 the total number of archdeaconries was reduced to two: Rochester and St. Albans forming one, and Essex the other. The extent and composition of the diocese was again entirely changed in 1877, when the new diocese of St. Albans was formed. Since that time the diocese of Rochester has included West Kent and part of Surrey, and has comprised three archdeaconries: Rochester, Kingston, and Southwark. In 1877 Danbury Palace had to be given up and Selsdon in Surrey became for a time the episcopal home. Quite recently a new palace has been completed at Kennington, in the most populous and needy part of the diocese.

In mediæval times the bishops of Rochester had a town house at Southwark. This was afterwards changed for the one at Lambeth Marsh, where the attempt to poison Bishop Fisher occurred. They had also other country homes at Halling and Trottescliffe. Our space will not, however, allow us to deal at length with these palaces outside the cathedral precincts.

The poverty of the Church at the time of the Conquest has been already mentioned, and even later we find that the episcopal revenue continued to be very small. One diocese only, we are told, paid a lower "Rome-scot," and only two English bishoprics appear as inferior in value in the King's books. Some old sources of episcopal and monastic income seem to us curious. The bulk was, of course, derived from manors or estates, but we find also that the bishop was entitled to a share of the whales killed on the shores of his diocese and that the monks of the priory of St. Andrew owned oyster fisheries. Out of the estates assigned to them the monks had to make an annual contribution, in kind, called the Xenium, to the bishop's income, and this, due on St. Andrew's Day, was on several occasions a subject of dispute. In Henry VIII.'s time we find the bishopric valued at £358 4s.

9½*d.*, and later, in 1595, it is stated that the clear annual profits did not exceed £220. To supplement this paltry revenue the bishops often held other appointments *in commendam*. During the latter part of the seventeenth century and the greater part of the eighteenth, the deanery of Westminster was, in this way, almost continuously attached to the bishopric of Rochester. Such pluralities are, of course, no longer allowed, the estates of this, as of other sees, being administered by the Ecclesiastical Commissioners, through whom the bishop receives the regular and more adequate income that he now enjoys. Poor though the see has been, we find many distinguished men among those who have held it. A great number of such passed on soon to richer bishoprics, and some even attained the archiepiscopal dignity, but one or two of the greatest consistently refused to be thus advanced.

THE GUILDHALL VANE

(From A Drawing By R. J. Beale).

For the sake of convenient reference, we now give a list of the bishops, in chronological order.

St. Justus, sent to reinforce the English mission in 601, became the first bishop in 604; fled to Gaul in 617, on the great relapse into idolatry after Ethelbert's death; summoned back after a year by the new king Eadbald; succeeded Mellitus as Archbishop of Canterbury in 624; died in 627.

Romanus, consecrated in 624; drowned while on a mission to Rome (*absorptus fluctibus Italici Maris*) probably in 627, but certainly before November, 630.

St. Paulinus came over with Justus; ordained Bishop of York, in 625, to accompany Ethelburga, princess of Kent, when she went to marry Edwin of Northumbria; baptised Edwin himself in April, 627, and earned well his title of the Apostle of Northumbria; preached also, we are told, in Lancashire, in Cumbria, on the Trent, and at Lincoln; fled with the widowed queen on Edwin's overthrow in 633, as he owed attendance to her; gladly received in Kent and persuaded to accept the see of Rochester, where, probably, he received the pallium sent him in 634; died in 644; buried in the *secretarium* of the church, whence his remains were afterwards transferred to the Norman cathedral.

St. Ythamar, the first bishop who was an Englishman by birth; died in 655; like Paulinus, buried in the church, and much revered, though the Normans seem to have been less eager to translate his remains.

Damian succeeded in 656, died in 664.

Putta succeeded five years later in 669; translated to Hereford in 676; died in 688.

Cuichelm resigned the see, through poverty, after only two years.

Gebmund, appointed in 678, died in 693.

Tobias, appointed in 693; famous for his great learning, which included a knowledge of both Greek and Latin; died in 726; buried in the *Porticus* of St. Paul, which he had himself built on to the cathedral.

Then came **Alduulf**, 726—d. 739 or 741; **Duina**, 741-747; **Earduulf**, 747 (or 757)-765; **Diora**, 778—d. 781; **Wermund**, 788-802; **Beornmod**, 803 (or 811)-814; **Tathnoth**, 841 (or 844)- ; **Godwin I.**; **Cutherwulf**, 868- ; **Swithulf**, 880- ; **Ruhric**; **Cheolmund**; **Chinefurth**; **Burrhic**; **Alfstan (Athelstan)**, 955- ; **Godwin II. (Godric)** and **Godwin III.**, c. 995—c. 1012. This is as complete a list as can be given until we come to Bishop Siward.

Siward was appointed in 1058; under him the establishment reached the greatest extreme of poverty, but, though it is suspected that the services of the church were also neglected, he was allowed to retain the see after the Conquest until his death in 1075.

Ernost, a monk, appointed by Lanfranc in 1076, died in the same year.

Gundulf, consecrated in 1077; came over with Lanfranc; also a great friend of Anselm; a skilful architect, rebuilt much of the cathedral, built the White Tower in London, St. Leonard's Tower and the nunnery at Malling, part of Dartford Church, and a tower at Rochester earlier than the present keep; substituted Benedictines for the old secular establishment of the cathedral; famous for piety and holiness, and in favour with the Conqueror and the two sons who succeeded him; died in 1108, aged 84; buried by Anselm in the cathedral, where a plain tomb is still called by his name.

Ralph d'Escures, an abbot of Sées who had been forced to flee by Robert of Bellême; a friend of Gundulf; some architectural work at Rochester carried out under his sway; Archbishop of Canterbury in 1114; died in 1122.

Ernulf came next in 1115; had been successively Prior of Canterbury and Abbot of Peterborough; built at both those places as well as at Rochester; famous for saintliness, and a great authority on canon law; perhaps best known generally by Sterne's comments in "Tristram Shandy" on the terrible excommunication curse contained in his "Textus Roffensis"; died in 1124.

John, formerly Archdeacon of Canterbury; Bishop of Rochester in 1125; cathedral consecrated in his time; died in 1137.

John, formerly Abbot of Sées; appointed in 1137; died in 1142.

Ascelin, succeeded in 1142; active bishop, even visited Rome for the monks of his cathedral; died in 1148.

Walter, chosen in 1148; the first bishop elected by the monks of the Priory of St. Andrew, the right being granted them by his brother Archbishop Theobald; formerly Archdeacon of Canterbury; died in 1182.

Gualeran, appointed in 1182; formerly Archdeacon of Bayeux; died in 1184.

Gilbert de Glanvill, consecrated in 1185; employed earlier by Becket on a mission to the Pope; quarrelled with his monks and helped Archbishops Baldwin and Hubert Walter (a friend of his own) against those of Canterbury; died 1214, before the Interdict was removed; buried at Rochester, where a tomb is shown as his.

Benedict de Sansetun, succeeded in 1215; saw cathedral plundered, and great works in new choir; died in 1226.

Henry Sandford; new choir entered in his first year, 1227; in a sermon at Sittingbourne said that the release from Purgatory, in one day, of Richard I., Stephen Langton, and a chaplain of the latter, had been revealed to him; died in 1235.

Richard de Wendover, not consecrated till 1238; monks had to appeal to Rome, against the archbishop's claims, to get their election of him confirmed; died in 1250.

Lawrence de Saint Martin, succeeded in 1251; appealed to Pope against a robbery of his see by Archbishop Boniface; at Rome for the canonization of St. William in 1256; died in 1274; his tomb (in the choir) has been described.

Walter de Merton, appointed in 1274; before this, chancellor (1261-63; 1272-74) and justiciar; founded his college at Maldon, and afterwards transferred it to Oxford; drowned in the Medway in 1277; buried in the cathedral (north choir transept).

John de Bradfield, a monk at Rochester; became bishop in 1277; died in 1283; buried in the cathedral (south choir aisle).

Thomas Inglethorp, appointed in 1283; formerly Dean of St. Paul's and Archdeacon of Middlesex; died in 1291; buried in the cathedral (chancel).

Thomas de Wouldham, Prior of Rochester, became bishop in 1292; died in 1317.

Hamo de Hythe, appointed in 1319 after a delay caused by Pope's wish to nominate John de Puteoli; did much for church and renewed the shrines of St. Paulinus and St. Ythamar; died in 1352; tomb in the cathedral (north choir aisle).

John de Sheppey, succeeded in 1352; treasurer of England, 1326-58; died in 1360; buried on the north side of the choir.

William of Whittlesea, Bishop of Rochester, 1362; of Worcester, 1364; Archbishop of Canterbury, 1368; died in 1374.

Thomas Trilleck, succeeded in 1364; formerly Dean of St. Paul's; died in 1372.

Thomas Brinton, appointed in 1373 by the Pope, who rejected the monk's nominee, their prior, John Hertley; a Benedictine of Norwich; had been penitentiary to the Roman see; died in 1389.

William de Bottisham, transferred from Llandaff in 1389, the Pope rejecting John Barnet; died in 1400.

John de Bottisham, succeeded in 1400; died in 1404; this repetition of the same surname has caused some confusion.

Richard Young, translated from Bangor in 1404; seems not to have taken full possession of see till 1407; died in 1418.

John Kemp, at earlier dates Keeper of Privy Seal and Chancellor of Normandy; Bishop of Rochester, 1419; of Chichester, 1421; of London, 1421; Archbishop of York, 1426; of Canterbury, 1452; Cardinal, 1439; prominent member of Beaufort party; Chancellor of England; served on several important political missions; died in 1454.

John Langdon, appointed in 1434; a royal councillor; author of an Anglorum Chronicon; died at Basle in 1434.

Thomas Brown, succeeded in 1435; in 1436, while still at Basle, translated by the Pope to Norwich; died in 1445.

William Wells, Abbot of York, succeeded in 1437; died before 26 February 1444.

John Lowe, translated from St. Asaph in 1444; English Provincial of the Order of St. Augustine; died in 1467; buried in north choir transept.

Thomas Rotheram (or **Scott**), appointed in 1468; translated to Lincoln, 1472; Archbishop of York, 1480; died in 1500; had been Chaplain to Edward IV., Keeper of the Privy Seal, and, in 1474, Lord Chancellor.

John Alcock succeeded in 1472; Privy Councillor, 1470-71; Lord Chancellor, 1474; first Lord President of Wales, 1476; tutor to Edward V., removed by Gloucester; under Henry VII., baptized Prince Arthur; comptroller of the royal works, and again Lord Chancellor; a great architect, works at Ely and Cambridge; translated to Worcester in 1476, to Ely in 1486; "devoted to learning and piety"; died in 1500.

John Russell, succeeded in 1476; translated to Lincoln, 1480; died in 1494.

Edmund Audley, Canon of York; Bishop of Rochester, 1480; of Hereford, 1492; of Salisbury, 1502; died in 1524; a legatee and executor of Henry VII.

Thomas Savage, Canon of York, Dean of the King's Chapel at Westminster; Bishop of Rochester, 1492, of London, 1496; Archbishop of York, 1501; died in 1507.

Richard FitzJames succeeded in 1496; translated to Chichester in 1503 and to London in 1506; died in 1522; a famous warden of Merton; Royal Almoner in 1495; did not favour Colet's efforts at reform.

John Fisher, having risen to the Chancellorship of Cambridge University in 1504, was then made, for his "grete and singular virtue," Bishop of Rochester; he and his patron, Lady Margaret, were great benefactors to Cambridge; a friend of Erasmus; opposed Henry VIII.'s divorce and the royal supremacy; made a cardinal just before he bravely and resignedly met his death in 1535.

John Hilsey came then in 1535; formerly Prior of the Dominicans in London; one of Cromwell's commissioners, compiled at his orders a service book in English; exposed the miraculous rood of Boxley at St. Paul's Cross; died in 1538.

Richard Heath, succeeded in 1539; had been Almoner to Henry VIII.; translated to Worcester, 1543; deprived for a time, but restored on Queen Mary's accession; Archbishop of York, 1555; Chancellor; held both the last appointments under Elizabeth, whose accession he proclaimed, but had to resign when the Act of Supremacy was enforced.

Henry Holbeach, succeeded in 1543; translated to Lincoln in 1546; previously suffragan Bishop of Bristol, and Prior (later Dean) of Worcester.

Nicholas Ridley, succeeded in 1547; translated to London when Bonner was removed in 1550; a famous Protestant, learned and pious; the story of his martyrdom with Latimer at Oxford, in 1555, is well known.

John Poynet, succeeded in 1550; translated to Winchester, 1551; left England when Mary became Queen; died at Strasburg in 1556.

John Scory, appointed in 1551; a great preacher; translated to Chichester in 1552; bishop of Hereford in 1559, when able to return from Friesland; died in 1585.

Maurice Griffith, appointed after an interval of about two years; educated by the Dominicans at Oxford; formerly Archdeacon of Rochester; one or two Protestants were burnt during his episcopacy; died in 1558.

Edmund Gheast, consecrated in 1559 and made Almoner to the Queen; transferred to Salisbury, 1571; died in 1578.

Edmund Freake, succeeded in 1571; previously Dean of Rochester, and of

Salisbury; Queen's Almoner in 1572; translated to Norwich in 1575, to Worcester in 1584; scandal at Norwich, his wife "will looke on him as the Divell lookes over Lincoln;" troubles with Puritans; died in 1590-91.

John Piers, succeeded in 1576; Bishop of Salisbury, 1577; Archbishop of York, 1589; Lord High Almoner, 1576; employed and consulted by the Queen; died in 1594.

John Yonge, became bishop in 1578; thought avaricious, but the annual revenue of his see shown not to exceed £220; died in 1605.

William Barlow, succeeded in 1605; wrote other works besides his account, denounced as partial by the Puritans, of the famous Hampton Court Conference; translated to Lincoln, 1608; died in 1613.

Richard Neile, succeeded in 1608; introduced Laud to the King's notice; Bishop of Lichfield, 1610, of Durham, 1617 and of Winchester, 1627; Archbishop of York, 1631; privy councillor; employed in famous Essex divorce case; sat in the courts of High Commission and of the Star Chamber; died in 1640.

John Buckeridge, formerly a canon at Rochester; confirmed as bishop in 1611; formerly a royal chaplain; took part in Essex case; active in religious discussions; translated to Ely, 1628; died in 1631.

Walter Curle, appointed in 1628; translated to Bath and Wells in 1629, to Winchester in 1632; deprived by Parliamentarians and apparently in great straits before he died, c. 1650.

John Bowle, appointed in 1629; apparently in ill-health, and consequently neglectful, for three years before his death in 1637.

John Warner, succeeded in 1638; seems to have been the last to struggle for his order's place in Parliament; deprived of revenues, but allowed to stay at Bromley under the Commonwealth; one of the nine bishops who lived till the Restoration; employed in the Savoy Conference; wealthy; benefactor to the cathedral and to Magdalen and Balliol Colleges, Oxford; founded college for clergymen's widows at Bromley; died in 1666; the last bishop buried in the cathedral.

John Dolben, made bishop in 1666; had served at Marston Moor and been wounded at York; retained his deanery of Westminster *in commendam*; translated to York in 1683; died in 1686.

Francis Turner, succeeded in 1683; translated to Ely in 1684; one of the seven bishops who petitioned against the Declaration of Indulgence, though he had been James II.'s chaplain; had to give up his see on account of his belief in James' divine right; died in 1700.

Thomas Sprat, Dean of Westminster, became Bishop of Rochester in 1685; of such literary ability as to have a place in Johnson's "Lives of the Poets;" wrote a poem on the death of Cromwell, a history of the Royal Society, a life of Cowley, etc.; in no great favour with William's government; implicated in the fabricated Flower-pot Plot, the papers concerning which were said to have been found in a flower-pot at Bromley; seems to have been somewhat of a time-server; died in

1713.

Francis Atterbury, born in 1662; took orders after the Revolution; became a Royal Chaplain, but still lived usually at Oxford; took part in the great controversy between Boyle and Bentley, on the Epistles of Phalaris; successively Archdeacon of Totnes, Dean of Carlisle, Dean of Christ Church, Oxford, and finally in 1713 Bishop of Rochester; in 1710 composed the speech for Sacheverell's defence before the House of Lords; a Tory, but, though he had tried to procure the proclamation of James III., he assisted at George I.'s coronation; deprived, for Jacobitism, of his see and banished in 1723; retired to Brussels and then for his health's sake to Paris; served James almost as a prime minister; in 1728 he left this service owing to bad treatment, but re-entered it before his death, after nine years of exile, in 1731-2.

Samuel Bradford, refused the see of St. David's in 1710; accepted that of Carlisle in 1718; translated to Rochester in 1723; in 1725 first dean of the revised Order of the Bath; his "Discourse concerning Baptismal and Spiritual Regeneration" (1709) had great popularity; died in 1731 at the Deanery, Westminster; buried in the Abbey.

Joseph Wilcocks, translated in 1731, from Gloucester, which see he had held since 1721; the new west front of Westminster Abbey finished in his time; he refused the Archbishopric of York before his death in 1756.

Zachary Pearce, succeeded in 1756; previously Dean of Winchester in 1739, and Bishop of Bangor in 1747; in 1768 he resigned the Deanery of Westminster, which he had held with his bishopric, but was not allowed to resign the see; died in 1774. While a fellow of Trin. Coll., Camb., he edited Longinus' works and Cicero's "De Oratore" and "De Officiis."

John Thomas was then bishop from 1774 until his death in 1793.

Samuel Horsley, born in 1733; a Fellow of the Royal Society in 1767, and one of its secretaries in 1773; Archdeacon of St. Alban's in 1782; resigned his membership of the Royal Society on account of the dispute, in 1783-4, with Sir Joseph Banks about its management; in 1785 he completed his edition of Newton's works; Prebendary of Gloucester, in 1787; Bishop of St. David's in 1788; translated to Rochester, with the deanery Westminster, in 1793, and thence to St. Asaph in 1802; died in 1806, showing his carelessness in money matters by letting a life policy for £5,000 lapse two days before his death; had engaged much in controversy with Priestley.

The Bishops of Rochester during this century have been **Thomas Dampier**, from 1802 to 1808, when he was translated to Ely; **Walter King**, from 1809 to 1827; **Hugh Percy**, appointed in 1827 but translated in the same year to Carlisle; **George Murray**, from 1827 to 1860; **Joseph Cotton Wigram**, from 1860 to 1867; **Thomas Legh Claughton**, from 1867 until his transfer to the new see of St. Alban's in 1877; **Anthony Wilson Thorold**, from 1877 until his translation to Winchester in 1891; **Dr. Randall Thomas Davidson**, who succeeded Dr. Thorold at Rochester, and again, on his death, at Winchester in 1895, and **Dr. Edward Stuart Talbot**, appointed in 1895, and still governing the diocese. These have all been worthy of their distinguished position and of their predecessors in the see.

Lector House believes that a society develops through a two-fold approach of continuous learning and adaptation, which is derived from the study of classic literary works spread across the historic timeline of literature records. Therefore, we aim at reviving, repairing and redeveloping all those inaccessible or damaged but historically as well as culturally important literature across subjects so that the future generations may have an opportunity to study and learn from past works to embark upon a journey of creating a better future.

This book is a result of an effort made by Lector House towards making a contribution to the preservation and repair of original ancient works which might hold historical significance to the approach of continuous learning across subjects.

HAPPY READING & LEARNING!

LECTOR HOUSE LLP
E-MAIL: lectorpublishing@gmail.com